Managing Performance Appraisal Systems

D1102560

B

Human Resource Management in Action Series

Series editor: Brian Towers

Other HRM books from Blackwell Business

MANAGING PERFORMANCE APPRAISAL SYSTEMS

GORDON C. ANDERSON

BLACKWELL
Oxford UK & Cambridge USA

First published 1993

Blackwell Publishers
108 Cowley Road
Oxford OX4 1JF
UK

238 Main Street, Suite 501
Cambridge, Massachusetts 02142
USA

British Library Cataloguing in Publication Data

A CIP catalogue record for this book is available from the British Library.

Library of Congress Cataloging-in-Publication Data

Anderson, Gordon C.
    Managing performance appraisal systems / Gordon C. Anderson.
        p.   cm. – (HRM in action)
    Includes bibliographical references and index.
    ISBN 0–631–18685–9 (pbk.: alk. paper)
    1. Employees – Rating of. I. Title. II. Series.
  HF5549.5.R3A529 1993
  658.3′ 125–dc20

Typeset in 11 on 13 pt Plantin
by Graphicraft Typesetters Ltd., Hong Kong
Printed in Great Britain by T.J. Press (Padstow) Ltd, Padstow, Cornwall

This book is printed on acid-free paper

Contents

List of Figures and Tables

Figures

Tables

Acknowledgements

My involvement in performance appraisal – as a researcher, consultant and business school teacher – extends over many years, and a large number of people have helped me in formulating my ideas on the subject. Although it generates many different points of view – supportive and hostile – performance appraisal is increasingly seen as making a valuable contribution to management. I hope that my interest and enthusiasm for this subject is communicated to the reader, even though I recognize there are many problems and issues to be addressed.

I have had the privilege of conducting seminars on this subject in many countries, and while much of the literature is American or British in origin, international interest in performance appraisal is increasing.

While addressing many performance appraisal issues, I have attempted to develop a different perspective from other books on the subject by focusing on the *management* of performance appraisal systems – an aspect of the subject apparently neglected in much of the literature.

For the development of this book I feel a deep sense of gratitude to the following:

My wife Marjory, and sons, Nigel and Christopher, for their encouragement, support and tolerance; Dr David Cameron, who for many years has generously given me the benefit of his knowledge and expertise in this subject; Miss Christine Reid, Head of the Business Information Centre in the Strathclyde Graduate Business School, for her ever-helpful and co-operative approach in helping me to find source materials; Robin Evenden, my co-author of *Management Skills: Making the Most of People*, from whom I have

Acknowledgements

learned a great deal about the human aspects of management; Fife Education Department, and in particular to Mr John C. McKeown, Assistant Director of Education, for encouragement and permission to use case study material relating to the Fife Staff Development and Appraisal Scheme for teachers; Scottish Nuclear Ltd, and in particular to Messrs John Kennedy, Ian Poad and David Carruthers, for permission to include a case study about the development of a new performance appraisal system in their organization; all of those individuals and organizations who have granted permission to include aspects of their work in this book; Richard Burton and David Kenning of Blackwell Publishers who helped me get underway with this book; Brian Towers, editor of the series, for suggesting the idea of the book to me in the first place; Jane Robertson and Sally Vince of Blackwell for their guidance and help in ensuring the rough edges in my manuscript were smoothed out in time for publication; and finally to Miss Gillian Watson, my secretary for three years, for her skill, hard work and cheerful support in undertaking the word processing of the whole of the manuscript while coping with many other duties.

Gordon C. Anderson
October 1992

Foreword

The observation that companies face increasingly intensive, global competition is now both commonplace and undoubtedly true. Even earth-girdling giants cannot guarantee their survival – as we have witnessed with IBM's first and massive loss in its corporate history. Nor can economies expect to ride on success forever, as current Japanese problems are perhaps indicating.

One consequence of the fight for survival and success is the now widespread realization within organizations that people are their most important asset. Cynics might say (including this one) that directors and senior managers should have realized this long ago although conversions, of the late variety, are always to be welcomed. This emphasis on the human resource implies that it also needs to be developed – and before that it has to be evaluated.

Performance appraisal systems are now widely recognized as a coherent approach towards evaluation and, increasingly, they are being applied to non-managerial as well as managerial employees. Yet surprisingly, whilst these systems are widespread little attention has been paid to their management. This book fills that gap.

Business history tells us to beware of new fads and panaceas and, inevitably, there are dangers in an uncritical and simplistic approach to the management of performance appraisal. Anderson draws upon US and UK organizational experience (as well as his own) to write the recipe for success in the implementation and management of performance appraisal. The ingredients include openness and the full involvement of employees (which could include their trade unions) and an awareness of the potential dangers in linking pay to performance. There is also the obvious requirement to ensure that employees are realistically and systematically helped to improve their performance through training and the popular, more individualistic approaches of counselling, coaching and monitoring.

All these aspects are discussed and considered in this book with the added bonus of two organizational case studies. Gordon Anderson brings together academic insight – honed in a business school environment – and a feel for the practical to introduce a book which will have wide appeal to academics and advanced students. It is also a book for practitioners; those actually managing performance appraisal systems, or thinking of introducing one, will find here much experience, sensible guidance and some comfort.

Brian Towers
Strathclyde Business School

Introduction

While a large literature has developed on the subject few, if any, books and articles have concentrated on the management of performance appraisal systems. Some writers, such as Maier (1958) and Burke, Weitzel & Weir (1978) have studied the interactions between appraisers and appraisees. Others, like, Randell, Packard & Slater (1984), have advocated a number of separate performance appraisal reviews, to fulfil different appraisal purposes. Latham & Wexley (1981) discuss problems in developing valid and reliable measures. Fletcher & Williams (1985), in a book that contains many insights into performance appraisal issues and linkages between performance appraisal and career development, devote one chapter to 'Devising and implementing appraisal systems'. In that chapter they identify, without much discussion, a number of areas of great importance to the effective management of performance appraisal systems. Mohrman, Resnick-West & Lawler (1989), in a major American book on the subject, provide a rigorous treatment of issues relating to the design of performance appraisal systems. The design phase is clearly an extremely important aspect – but it is only one aspect – in the total process of managing performance appraisal systems.

This book aims both at integrating and updating many aspects of performance appraisal, while concentrating on the hitherto neglected subject of the management of performance appraisal systems. In many books and articles on performance appraisal, there is a marked division, particularly between UK and US writers who have a tendency to draw largely on the literature findings from their own country. This book aims to overcome this divide by drawing in a balanced way on British and American sources, and also on theory and practice from elsewhere, since there is evidence of growing interest in performance appraisal in many countries across different continents.

This book aims to provide a comprehensive coverage of the management of performance appraisal systems, and is aimed primarily at meeting the needs of academics, practitioners and students with a particular interest in this subject. It is envisaged that it could be used by students taking advanced courses in human resource management, at undergraduate, post-graduate, professional and post-experience levels. It is particularly hoped that the book will assist human resource managers, training managers, and managers from other functions who have an involvement in performance appraisal, in bringing about better-managed performance appraisal systems in organizations. It will also be of interest to internal and external consultants who, in addressing management problems and change processes, must consider appraisal issues.

References

Burke, R.J., Weitzel, W. and Weir, T. 1978: Characteristics of Effective Employee Performance Review and Development Interviews: Replication and Extension. *Personnel Psychology*, 31 (3), 903–918.

Fletcher, C.A. and Williams, R. 1985: *Performance Appraisal and Career Development*. London: Hutchinson.

Latham, G.P. and Wexley, K.N. 1981: *Increasing Productivity Through Performance Appraisal*. Reading, Mass.: Addison Wesley.

Maier, N.R.F. 1958: *The Appraisal Interview*. New York: John Wiley.

Mohrman, A.M., Resnick-West, S.M. and Lawler, E.E. 1989: *Designing Performance Appraisal Systems*. San Francisco: Jossey-Bass.

Randell, G., Packard, P. and Slater, J. 1984: *Staff Appraisal: A First Step to Effective Leadership* revised edn., London: IPM.

1

Performance Appraisal: The Wider Context and Emerging Trends

All organizations must face up to the challenge of how to evaluate, utilize and develop the skills and abilities of their employees to ensure that organizational goals are achieved, and also to ensure that individuals gain as much satisfaction as possible from their jobs while making effective contributions. As competition in many markets becomes more intense and global in nature, it is hardly surprising that an increasing number of organizations are recognizing the importance of performance appraisal as a key element of human resource management.

While Guest (1989) rightly points out that the term human resource management (HRM) can mean different things to different people, the modern concept suggests the emergence of a consensus view that there is, or should be, increased emphasis on a more strategic and integrated approach to HRM in organizations. This implies that considerable attention should be paid to HRM considerations in the formulation of corporate strategy. Sissons (1989) puts forward the view that the management of people is a key, probably *the* key element, in the strategic planning of any business. Developing this theme, Connock (1991) argues not only the importance of HRM, but also the need for a human resource vision, including a philosophy of how to treat people in the organization, and the importance of people to the organization, suggesting this human resource vision should be a fundamental component of 'first-order' business strategies.

A statement of mission is needed in any organization to provide a focus for setting business objectives, and developing an appropriate structure. Drucker (1974) has for many years been emphasizing how important it is for all types of business enterprise to face up to the questions 'What business are we in? . . . What business should we be in?' to ensure that a worthwhile mission statement is formulated. The mission statement implies the need for a future vision of what the business is expected to be at some defined point in the future.

Strategy is concerned with the formulation of the long-term business goals to permit the future vision of the business to be realized, and the adoption of courses of action for the allocation of resources necessary for achieving these goals.

The probability of success in achieving strategic goals will depend on a number of factors, including the culture of the organization, which will play an important part in how the organization moves from where it is now to where it wants to be in the future in order to achieve its strategic goals. Culture in this context refers to the system of values, norms and behaviour throughout the organization.

In developing its culture, the organization needs to consider:

- how people relate to organizational objectives
- how people interact with one another
- how people develop values and beliefs supportive to the achievement of strategic goals
- how people are rewarded
- how the performance of people is evaluated and developed.

This last point suggests that a system of performance appraisal can make an important contribution to cultural change and to the development of appropriate cultures in organizations.

Probably the most widely used approaches in the formulation of strategy are based on the writings of Michael Porter (1980) who has stressed the importance of a methodical approach in analysing a range of internal and external factors, to help organizations position themselves effectively in a competitive environment. Hendry, Pettigrew & Sparrow (1988) have found evidence to support the view that greater awareness of competitive pressures has made more companies take into account HRM considerations in formulating strategy.

Strategic HRM is concerned with the planning, management,

control, evaluation and development of the people resources of an organization, in order to derive as much value-added as possible. Guest (1989) has argued that a number of conditions must be fulfilled for strategic HRM to flourish in any organization. These include:

- support from top management
- a strong culture which reinforces human resource management
- a conscious strategy to achieve business success through the full and effective utilization of human resources
- an ability to get HRM policies into place.

Systems for evaluating, rewarding and developing the human resources of the organizations lie at the heart of human resource management. Performance appraisal is now widely regarded as an essential element of effective HRM in organizations.

Trends in the use of Performance Appraisal

Increasing recognition of the widespread use of performance appraisal has been confirmed in a number of major surveys. In the UK, for example, three large national surveys of performance appraisal practices have been carried out by the Institute of Personnel Management (IPM). The first of these surveys (Gill, Ungerson & Thakur, 1973) drew upon 360 UK-based organizations from a wide range of sectors in industry, commerce and the public service. Of the responding organizations, 74 per cent indicated they were operating some kind of formalized performance appraisal scheme, while 26 per cent did not. The second IPM study (Gill, 1977) also covered a large representative sample of 288 UK-based organizations, of whom 82 per cent reported they were operating performance appraisal schemes while 18 per cent did not. A similar percentage (82 per cent) in the third and most recent IPM survey (Long, 1986), which had 306 responding organizations, indicated they were operating appraisal schemes. In this study, substantial increases in the coverage of systems of performance appraisal for non-managerial employees were reported. For example, 55 per cent of those organizations surveyed reported the inclusion in their systems of performance appraisal of non-managerial 'knowledge' workers – employees who provide professional, scientific and advisory services. This study also provided evidence that many more organizations included secretarial, clerical and manual employees in their schemes.

Similar US surveys have demonstrated how widely established performance appraisal practices are in US organizations. For example a study by the Bureau of National Affairs (1983) highlighted 91 per cent of a sample of 244 US organizations operating systems of performance appraisal.

A number of trends can be detected from some of the surveys, which must be taken into account in considering the management of performance appraisal systems. In particular, drawing upon the most recent of the three IPM surveys, the following trends can be noted.

Towards more openness

Totally closed systems, in which individuals do not see, or have any access to their own appraisal reports, have become extremely rare. Most systems have in-built procedures to ensure that employees have the opportunity to see their completed reports. Typically, the signatures of appraisees are required, to ensure that processes and appraisal outcomes are open to appraisers and appraisees alike. Some systems remain semi-open, where reports about the future potential of individuals are treated as confidential, the reasoning being that confidentiality is assumed to lead to more candid, honest predictions of future potential. In addition, it can be argued that if such reports were open, individuals might become demotivated if the reports were unflattering. On the other hand, if the reports are positive about their potential and promotability, there is an additional danger of overraising expectations, with individuals being inclined to confuse plans with promises, and becoming disillusioned with the organization if the plans regarding their future do not materialize. Other organizations, however, reject this reasoning, suggesting that if there is to be total honesty and high levels of trust, all aspects of the appraisal process should be open.

Towards greater employee participation

An increasing number of organizations are attempting to introduce and develop procedures within their systems of performance appraisal to ensure that employees being appraised are encouraged to participate actively in the process. A number of approaches can be developed:

- Training appraisers to be participative in their style of conducting appraisal interviews.
- Introducing appraisal interview preparation forms, to be completed by appraisees, prior to appraisal interviews.
- More ambitiously, building an element of self-analysis and self-appraisal into appraisal interview preparation documents, and encouraging appraisers to invite appraisees to undertake self-appraisal at appraisal interviews.

The inclusion of greater elements of employee participation in performance appraisal systems has been a major development, especially during the 1980s, and research evidence (e.g. Wexley, Singh and Yukl, 1973) has for long been pointing out the benefits.

Towards results-oriented systems

A high proportion of organizations emphasize, through their appraisal documentation, the setting of objectives, and the evaluation of performance against these objectives at the end of a time period, typically a year or six months, as the basis for performance appraisal. The development of objective-based systems has largely been at the expense of traditional trait-oriented schemes in which managers assess employees on a range of personality traits.

Towards composite schemes

Long (1986) has identified that more organizations are developing composite appraisal schemes, using a range of different approaches and criteria to evaluate performance, while often placing the emphasis primarily, as noted above, on results-oriented methods. This strategy helps to ensure that not only outcomes or results but also the processes involved in reaching results are assessed. As Mayo (1991) points out, '... to assess only the results themselves is not sufficient – we need to analyse why objectives were achieved or not achieved, and this leads us into the person's strengths and weaknesses'.

Towards wider ownership

The 'ownership' of performance appraisal systems has shifted increasingly towards the line managers and the employees – the key parties involved as appraisers and appraisees. This shift is very much in line with current thinking about the evolution of HRM which increasingly places the responsibility for human resource decisions, including those relating to the evaluation, development and rewarding of individuals, with line mangers. Personnel and training specialists still have important roles to play in being champions for the establishment of sound appraisals, and in the management of performance appraisal systems on an ongoing basis. If line managers are given ownership, it is likely they will show much greater commitment to performance appraisal than if the system is seen to be owned by personnel and training specialists, a practice that has often occurred in the past. This implies wide consultation in the initial design phase, and in the formative stages, to ensure not only that as many line managers as possible are kept fully briefed about developments, but that they are also encouraged to contribute ideas and suggestions to the design of the performance appraisal system.

Towards coverage of more categories of employees

As well as becoming more widely used in all types of organizations, there is evidence that performance appraisal is being extended to cover more employee groups – in some cases, all employees. Long (1986) provides evidence that organizations have been extending their systems of performance appraisal to include more employees at all levels of the hierarchy – from directors to clerical and manual workers. With the substantially increased coverage of various groups of non-managerial employees, many organizations have introduced several variants of their performance appraisal systems (see, e.g. Anderson, Hulme and Young, 1987).

As a central element of performance management

Performance management as emphasized by Pocock (1991), is increasingly seen as an holistic process that should be interpreted broadly to include a range of strategies, firmly set within the context of business strategy, for developing the performance of all people in the organization. Performance appraisal has a central part to play in encouraging performance management, in ensuring that the performance of individuals is accurately and fairly evaluated as a basis for a range of strategies for rewarding employees, and developing their performance through coaching, counselling and training.

References

Anderson, G.C., Hulme, D. and Young, E. 1987: Appraisal without forms. *Personnel Management*, February.

Bureau of National Affairs 1983: *Performance Appraisal Programs*. Washington, DC: The Bureau (Personnel Policies Forum Survey 135).

Connock, S. 1991: *HR Vision: Managing a Quality Workforce*. London: IPM.

Drucker, P.F. 1974: *Management: Tasks, Responsibilities, Practices*. London: Heinemann.

Gill, D. 1977: *Appraising Performance: Present Trends and the Next Decade*. London: IPM.

Gill, D., Ungerson, B. and Thakur, M. 1973: *Performance Appraisal in Perspective: A Survey of Current Practice*. London: IPM.

Guest, D. 1989: Personnel and HRM: Can You Tell the Difference? *Personnel Management*, January.

Hendry, C., Pettigrew, A. and Sparrow, P. 1988: Changing Patterns of Human Resource Management. *Personnel Management*, November.

Long, P. 1986: *Performance Appraisal Revisited*. London: IPM.

Mayo, A. 1991: *Managing Careers: Strategies for Organisations*. London: IPM.

Pocock, P. 1991: Introduction. In Neale, F. (ed.), *The Handbook of Performance Management*. London: IPM.

Porter, M. 1980: *Competitive Strategy: Techniques for Analysing Industries and Competition*. London: Collier McMillan.

Sissons, K. (ed.) 1989: *Personnel Management in Britain*. Oxford: Blackwell.

Wexley, K.N., Singh, J.P. and Yukl, G.A. 1973: Subordinate personality as a moderator of the effects of participation in three types of appraisal interviews. *Journal of Applied Psychology*, 58 (1).

2

Identifying the Objectives of Performance Appraisal

A necessary condition for the effective management of performance appraisal systems in any organization is the need to clarify and communicate to all concerned the objectives which the system is intended to achieve. Typically, performance appraisal schemes are expected to serve multiple objectives. This can often be a strength in that several purposes can be achieved, but it can also prove to be a disadvantage if it leads to a dissipation of effort and lack of focus. It is obviously of crucial importance, and everyone in an organization – and especially the key decision-makers – should be fully aware precisely what objectives the system of performance appraisal is expected to achieve, and the priorities within these objectives.

Case study

A major UK engineering company was recently considering the introduction of a new performance appraisal scheme. Ninety-one senior managers were each given a list of possible objectives for a system of performance appraisal and asked to place them in rank order in terms of importance, from 1 (highest) to 7 (lowest). The seven objectives selected by the company for this exercise are broadly typical of those set by many organizations for their performance appraisal schemes. The managers' rankings are shown in Table 2.1. As can easily be seen, there is an enormous diversity of views, with each of the objectives receiving both top rankings and bottom rankings. This kind of result is by no means untypical of that found for exercises of this sort carried out by other organizations, and it highlights the necessity for spending time, in the initial phases of

Table 2.1 Ranking of the objectives of performance appraisal by ninety-one senior managers in a large UK engineering company

| | Number & percentage of respondents | | | | | | |
| | | | Ranks | | | | |
Objectives	1	2	3	4	5	6	7
To monitor past performance against agreed standards.	26 29%	13 14%	14 15%	17 19%	5 5%	8 9%	8 9%
To identify training and development needs.	19 21%	19 21%	16 18%	16 18%	13 14%	6 7%	2 2%
To improve future work performance.	26 29%	18 20%	15 16%	7 8%	9 10%	14 15%	2 2%
To help the company make decisions on pay.	7 8%	6 7%	15 16%	13 14%	5 5%	13 14%	32 35%
To provide opportunities for employees to discuss their ambitions with their managers.	9 10%	16 18%	21 23%	13 14%	19 21%	5 5%	8 9%
To identify employee potential.	19 21%	22 24%	17 19%	9 10%	9 10%	10 11%	5 5%
To give individuals feedback from their managers on how they are performing.	24 26%	16 18%	9 10%	15 16%	11 12%	9 10%	7 8%

designing and setting up systems of performance appraisal, to consult widely with members of the organization, and to discuss thoroughly possible objectives and how they should be prioritized. Having reached a decision it is important that the objectives set for the performance appraisal system and the priorities among these objectives are clearly communicated to those involved.

The process used by this engineering company is also of significance. Wide consultation in the early design phase not only generates interest and understanding of what objectives might be set, but also is likely to lead to greater commitment to performance appraisal on the part of those involved. This should never be underestimated.

Objectives of Performance Appraisal

Performance appraisal objectives can be classified in a number of ways. One of the best known classifications was produced many years ago by McGregor (1960) who groups them in three ways:

Administrative – providing an orderly way of determining promotions, transfers and salary increases.

Informative – supplying data to management on the performance of subordinates and to the individual on his or her strengths and weaknesses.

Motivational – creating a learning experience that motivates staff to develop themselves and improve their performance.

McGregor's groupings are useful in drawing attention not only to the variety of purposes but also to different organizational philosophies towards performance appraisal.

Cummings and Schwab (1973) adopt a different perspective. They contend that organizations typically view appraisal as having two broad purposes: an evaluative function, and a development function.

The evaluative function

The evaluative function of performance appraisal is in reviewing past performance in the light of what has been achieved: actual performance is assessed in relation to what is seen as desired performance.

This function corresponds closely to McGregor's administrative category. Data are generated and used as a basis for making decisions on promotions, transfers and salary increases, although this latter purpose is one of the more controversial areas and is discussed in detail in chapter 9. American studies typically regard salary decisions as being central to performance appraisal and crucial to its credibility. British writers have often emphasized the dangers of too close a link causing the salary issue to overshadow all aspects, to the detriment of the other useful purposes of performance appraisal.

While it may be logical for performance appraisal and salary decisions to be linked, there should be a separation in time and in procedure between appraisal systems and salary review systems.

The development function

For the development function of appraisal, concentration is on improving the performance of people by identifying areas for improvement, setting performance targets for the future, and agreeing plans for follow-up action. This aspect also involves developing the capacity of people through formulating plans to develop their skills and careers; helping individuals to reconcile their job and career aspirations with opportunities available in the organization.

Furthermore, there is a certain amount of overlap between the evaluative and development functions, in that the evaluation of past performance will often be an important influence upon the setting of future targets. Brinkerhoff and Kanter (1980) contend that this function is both backward-looking – in the sense of evaluating past performance so as to establish standards – and forward-looking – in that the established standards serve as incentives for future performance improvement through generating peer competition and the desire to beat one's own past record.

TOM ?

They argue further that an additional overlapping, but also overarching purpose for performance appraisal, is to ensure that managers are performing a critical management function. Managers should be paying careful attention to the assessment of the past performance of their staff against organizational requirements, and to the development of greater productivity of the human resources available. In my experience, this function of performance appraisal – of encouraging careful and systematic approaches in assessing the performance of employees – is of great importance for practising managers, and its value is often recognized by them.

The possible conflict between the evaluative and developmental dimensions has been much discussed in the appraisal literature. The central issue would appear to be: can the manager, acting as appraiser, effectively be both judge and helper without experiencing role conflict? Since future decisions must be based, at least in part, on evaluations of previous behaviour, it could be argued that this conflict is superficial rather than real, and that an effective manager should be able to cope effectively with both roles.

Mohrman, Resnick-West and Lawler (1989) argue, however, that individual employees may have conflicting objectives in being appraised, especially where performance appraisal is strongly linked with the extrinsic rewards they receive. The argument is that employees will place great emphasis on presenting themselves and their performance in the most favourable way possible to their appraisers, because they realize that the results of performance appraisal will have a substantial influence on the extrinsic rewards (especially pay) which they will receive. They will tend to deny problems, attribute areas of deficient performance to others, and claim all aspects of successful performance have been due to their own skills and efforts.

Employees being appraised will wish not only to maximize extrinsic rewards, but also, according to Meyer, Kay and French (1965), to gain accurate and helpful feedback about their performance. They will recognize the benefit of constructive discussions with their appraisers to analyse performance problems, remove barriers to performance improvement and agree plans for personal development and higher levels of performance in the future. Thus an area of conflict among the objectives of the employee occurs: whether to be very open and candid in providing information, parts of which may be unfavourable, in order to receive the feedback they need for growth and development, or whether to withhold some information which they feel could lead to negative interpretations about their performance in order to obtain good extrinsic rewards.

Conflicts between organizational and individual objectives can also occur, as articulated by Porter, Lawler and Hackman (1975), and shown in a diagram adapted from Mohrman, Resnick-West and Lawler (1989) (see figure 2.1). The conflict between individual and organizational objectives centres around the fact that to achieve its purposes the organization needs comprehensive and valid data about the performance of its employees, but it may not be in the interests of individuals to provide this information if it is seen to impact on their external rewards.

It is easy to overstate the extent to which these conflicts occur among appraisal objectives, especially in the case of high performers. Where unfavourable aspects of performance are slight, the impediments of the interchange of information between appraisers and appraisees are minimal. In dealing with marginal or deficient performers, the conflicts discussed can be a major factor which must be taken into account.

The culture of the organization, and in particular the extent to

Figure 2.1 Conflicts inherent in performance appraisal

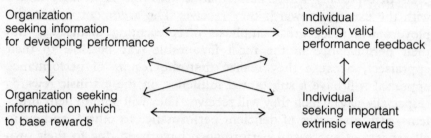

Organization
seeking information
for developing performance

Individual
seeking valid
performance feedback

Organization seeking
information on which
to base rewards

Individual
seeking important
extrinsic rewards

Source: Adapted from Mohrman, Resnick-West and Lawler (1989)

which relationships are characterized by openness and mutual trust, clearly affect appraisal relationships. Many organizations, to minimize the possibility of conflict among appraisal objectives, are increasingly placing emphasis on climate-setting. They are encouraging managerial styles that will lead to openness and frankness in relationships, as a condition for establishing an effective performance appraisal system. The relationship between organization culture and performance appraisal systems is being increasingly recognized as two-way, and Holdsworth (1991) has drawn attention to the modern trend of organizations using their performance appraisal systems to being about cultural change.

Empirical data about performance appraisal systems and their objectives have been gathered and analysed in a number of surveys. Gill (1977) and Long (1986) have identified the main purposes of performance appraisal in two studies carried out by the IPM in the UK. These were both large-scale surveys covering a representative spread of organizations from all sectors of industry, commerce and the public service. There were 288 responding organizations in the earlier of the two surveys in 1977, and 310 in the 1986 survey. The results are compared in table 2.2. The most significant change between the 1977 and 1986 findings has been the substantial increase in the number of organizations that relate the setting of performance objectives to the appraisal process. This implies that many of the organizations have redesigned their systems of performance appraisal to include a different mix, or a different emphasis in the methods and criteria used. These are more fully discussed in a later chapter.

Table 2.2 The main purpose of performance appraisal schemes as identified by UK companies

Major purpose	Percentage of companies	
	1977[a] (*n* = 288)	*1986*[b] (*n* = 310)
To assess training needs	96	97
To improve current performance	92	97
To review past performance	91	98
To assess future potential	87	71
To assist career planning decisions	81	75
To set performance objectives	57	81
To assess salary increases	39	40

Sources: [a]Gill (1977) and [b]Long (1986)

As is clearly evident from table 2.2, most, indeed almost all, organizations view their performance appraisal systems as being centrally concerned with identifying the training and development needs of employees, reviewing their past performance and improving their current performance.

There has been a shift away from using performance appraisal to assess the future potential and promotability of employees, even though a large number of organizations (71 per cent) still record this as one of their appraisal purposes. A number of factors may help to explain this downward shift of emphasis:

1. Increased dissatisfaction with very subjective, simplistic ways of encouraging line managers to rate the future potential of their staff, included in some systems of performance appraisal.
2. A lower rate of economic growth in the UK during the decade between these surveys, leading to organizations being more interested in the current performance of employees, and less interested in their future potential, at a time when fewer promoted posts were becoming available.
3. The increased recognition and use of assessment centres in providing different mechanisms for assessing employees' future potential.
4. Changing patterns in organizational design. Many organizations appear to be following the approaches advocated by Handy (1989) and Kanter (1989) in moving towards more flexible, flatter organization structures,

with fewer levels in the organization hierarchy. Again this leads, and will lead, increasingly to greater emphasis on performance in the current job, and less emphasis on identifying the future potential of employees if, for reasons of organizational design, promoted posts are to be few in number.

It would be wrong to suggest from this that organizations can legitimately ignore issues concerned with identifying the future potential of employees. The message is rather that this is an area of challenge in the design and operation of performance appraisal systems. It can be reasonably argued that as competitive forces in many markets become more intense and global, new approaches are required in identifying and utilizing the future potential of employees. Using performance appraisals to assist with career planning decisions is seen as an important purpose, stressing the counselling and advisory dimension of appraisals.

Probably the most surprising statistic is the apparent absence of change in terms of interest in relating the results of performance appraisal to pay decisions. There is other evidence to suggest, however, that this, while still a controversial issue in some quarters, is a matter of growing organizational importance and is discussed in depth in chapter 9.

A major challenge for any organization is to make clear to all concerned what it regards as the key purposes of its performance appraisal scheme. Without this clarification, the experience of a number of companies suggests that performance appraisal often degenerates into a ritualistic process, perceived by those involved as a meaningless, paper-filling exercise that bears little resemblance to what people actually do and to real issues in the organization.

The Benefits of Performance Appraisal

As well as specifying the purposes of performance appraisal, it is important to clarify what performance appraisal means to each of the main parties involved, in terms of what they can expect to gain.

Who are the main parties? They can be defined as:

- The appraisee, i.e. the person being appraised.
- The appraiser, the manager conducting the appraisal.
- The organization.

Assuming appraisals are properly carried out, appraisees benefit in terms of:

- greater clarity of the results/standards expected of them;
- accurate and constructive feedback on past performance;
- greater knowledge of strengths and weaknesses;
- the development of plans to improve on performance by building on strengths and minimizing as far as possible weaknesses;
- an opportunity to communicate upwards views and feelings about the job and the utilization of the appraisee's skills in the job;
- a clearer view of the context of the job by learning about the manager's objectives and priorities for the section/department/division;
- discussion of career prospects.

Given the natural anxieties that most people have when their work is being appraised, and their competence is under scrutiny, it is extremely important that all managers who conduct appraisal should recognize the need and accept the responsibility to communicate these benefits as clearly as possible to their staff. Only if staff perceive the benefits outweighing their natural apprehensions about appraisal, can they reasonably be expected to participate fully, and without feelings of defensiveness, in performance appraisal.

Appraisers can expect to gain the following benefits if they carry out appraisals in a thorough and conscientious manner:

- the opportunity to measure and identify trends in performance of staff;
- better understanding of staff, their fears, anxieties, hopes and aspirations;
- the opportunity of clarifying the appraiser's own objectives and priorities, with a view to giving staff a better view of how their contribution fits in with the work of others;
- enhanced motivation of staff, by focusing attention on them as individuals;
- developing staff performance;
- identifying opportunities for rotating or changing the duties of staff.

These benefits constitute the objectives of good management. A major challenge is, therefore, the communication of this message to appraisers to encourage them to view performance appraisal as an essential element of good management and as a mechanism which, if properly implemented, increases the likelihood that the appraiser's own objectives will be achieved.

It is important to recognize that the organization as a whole, and not just individuals, benefits from a carefully implemented performance appraisal scheme. Benefits that accrue to the organization include:

- improved communications
- generally enhanced motivation of staff
- the greater harmonization of objectives
- and above all, improved corporate performance.

The simple, but fundamentally important issue of talking through with the key parties involved, and helping them to clarify the benefits they can reasonably expect to derive from performance appraisal is one of the essential foundations upon which a system of performance appraisal can be built. This process, if carried out effectively, is likely to assist in resolving the possible conflicts among appraisal objectives to which reference has previously been made, and in gaining the commitment of all parties to performance appraisal.

If the initial phase is not undertaken, the danger will exist to a greater extent that:

- Appraisees will feel apprehensive about being appraised, and will behave defensively.
- Appraisers will devote little time and effort to performance appraisal, reducing it to a meaningless ritualistic exercise.
- Top management in the organization will fail to show enthusiasm for it, and to give it their wholehearted support.

If any or all of these problems materialize, it is unlikely that the many useful objectives that systems of performance appraisal can achieve will be realized.

References

Brinkerhoff, D.W. and Kanter, R.M. 1980: Appraising the Performance of Performance Appraisal. *Sloan Management Review*, Spring.

Cummings, L.L. and Schwab, D. 1973: *Performance in Organisations: Determinants and Appraisals*. Glenview, IL: Scott Foresman.

Gill, D. 1977: *Appraising Performance*. London: IPM.

Handy, C. 1989: *The Age of Unreason*. London: Business Books.

Holdsworth, R. 1991: Appraisal. In F. Neale. (ed.), *Performance Management*. London: IPM.

Kanter, R.M. 1989: *When Giants Learn to Dance*. London: Simon & Schuster.

Long, P. 1986: *Performance Appraisal Revisited*. London: IPM.

McGregor, D. 1960: *The Human Side of Enterprise*. New York: McGraw-Hill.

Meyer, H.H., Kay, E. and French, J.P.R. 1965: Split Roles in Performance Appraisal. *Harvard Business Review*, 43.

Mohrman, A.L., Resnick-West, S.M. and Lawler, E.E. 1989: *Designing Performance Appraisal Systems*. San Francisco: Jossey-Bass.

Porter, L.W., Lawler, E.E. and Hackman, J.R. 1975: *Behaviour in Organisations*. New York: McGraw-Hill.

3
Evaluating Appraisal Options

In developing performance appraisal systems a critical decision concerns the appraisal method to adopt. A large number of methods can be, and indeed are, used by organizations, and the main options are described and evaluated in this chapter.

The first part of the chapter looks at seven methods that to a large extent rely upon the appraiser's judgement. The second part of the chapter looks at six further methods that assess and analyze an appraisee's performance, using more objective forms of evaluation.

Methods that Depend Primarily on the Appraiser's Judgement and Viewpoint

A number of long-established techniques used in systems of performance include:

- Alphabetical/numerical rating.
- Forced choice rating, including forced choice rating indices.
- Personality trait rating.
- Graphic rating scale.
- Forced distribution.
- Ranking.
- Paired comparisons.

While differing widely, they have the common feature that all place a high degree of reliance on the subjective judgement of the appraiser. 'Subjective' here refers to the danger that an appraiser's judgement will be influenced by his or her own viewpoint rather than by the actual characteristic or situation being appraised. For this reason, these methods are less commonly used in organizations nowadays, although they are still found – in their entirety or as one element of a composite approach. A brief description and examples of each follow.

Alphabetical/numerical rating

The appraiser is asked to rate employees on a number of different work qualities such as:

- Quantity and quality of work.
- Job knowledge.
- Problem-solving ability.

A simple rating scale (e.g. high–low, 1–5 or A–E) permits discrimination between better and worse areas of performance. Figure 3.1 shows a typical rating scale. This approach is easily understood, and appraisers can complete the documentation rapidly. It suffers, however, from the problems of rater bias (i.e. of the person doing the rating) and of central tendency (giving marks in the middle of the range and avoiding the extremes). Furthermore, each appraiser is likely to interpret differently factors such as decision-making, relationships with subordinates, etc.

Forced choice rating

This method uses a number of adjectives or phrases to indicate higher or lower performance. The appraiser is asked to identify the adjectives or phrases that best describe the performance of each employee. Alternatively the appraiser is asked to indicate those adjectives or phrases that least well describe the employee's performance. Figure 3.2 gives an example of forced choice rating.

This approach is seldom used in practice because of the substantial amount of development work required. Preparation involves research into the characteristics of high and low performers in each job or occupational group, as a basis for developing the statements to be included in the appraisal document. Considerable effort is needed to analyse the results of completed appraisal forms. As you can see in the example, two statements in each of the three groups are unfavourable; the same number are favourable.

Forced choice rating index

An index has to be computed for each employee, based on the number of favourable/unfavourable statements that have been selected as being representative of work performance.

Considering and presenting index values is an important aspect of the design work. An extremely simple scoring system might assign

Figure 3.1   Example of alphabetical/numerical ratings

Instruction to appraiser
Using the 5-point scale below, please place a tick in the column which most closely represents your view of the level of employee performance for each element.

Assessment of Current Performance	High 1 A	2 B	3 C	4 D	Low 5 E
Knowledge of present duties		√			
Planning ability			√		
Skill in implementing work plans			√		
Decision-making ability			√		
Accuracy of work				√	
Ability to communicate orally			√		
Ability to communicate in writing				√	
Willingness to accept new ideas		√			
Problem-solving ability			√		
Relationships with superiors		√			
Relationships with peers		√			
Relationships with subordinates	√				
Relationships with clients			√		

Source: Anderson (1986)

zero scores to negative statements, and different, in this case positive, scores to favourable statements, according to how the organization perceives their desirability. In figure 3.2, therefore, the employee would score a zero in the second section through being identified as 'over-confident'. If, say, positive scores of 3 and 4 were attached to the qualities 'knows how and when to delegate' and 'admits

Figure 3.2   Example of a forced choice rating

Instruction to appraiser
Statements about work performance are arranged in groups of four. For each group of statements tick which is most representative of, and which is least representative of the employee being assessed.

	Most	*Least*
Unwilling to assume responsibility		
Knows how and when to delegate responsibility	√	
Offers useful suggestions		
Too easily changes his/her ideas		√
Over-confident	√	
Inspires pride in the organization		
Lacks tact		
Thoughtful of others		√
Criticizes organizational policies		√
Others experience difficulty in working with him/her		
Admits mistakes when wrong	√	
Others know they can rely on his/her judgement		

Source: Anderson (1986)

mistakes when wrong' respectively, the employee would have gained a score of 7 for those ratings.

Employees would ultimately be ranked in terms of their overall scores: the higher the score the greater the performance level achieved.

The advantage of this approach is that errors of central tendency, strictness and leniency tend to be reduced by removing scale values. The drawbacks are not only the time and effort required to devise and analyse appraisals and weightings but also the problem of standardizing appraisers' interpretations of the phrases and adjectives used, such as: confidence, tact, fair, average.

Personality trait rating

A structured form is used requiring the appraiser to rate each employee on a scale containing usually four, five or six points on a number of personal qualities and personality characteristics such as: confidence, enthusiasm, maturity, steadiness under pressure, initiative. On some forms an attempt is made to define the characteristics that have to be assessed. Although this method may highlight important aspects of employee performance and potential, it suffers the disadvantages that many appraisers may find it difficult to agree common interpretations of the personality factors, and may be reluctant to embark upon the process of assessing employees' personalities. An example of this approach is shown in figure 3.3.

Graphic rating scale

The appraiser is asked, as shown in figure 3.4, to rate employees in terms of a number of defined work or personal qualities by placing a tick somewhere along a line from 'very high' to 'very low'. The principal advantages of this method are:

- its relative simplicity
- ease of comprehension
- avoidance of having to slot people into specific categories.

The disadvantages are the problems of

- central tendency
- rater bias
- meaning or interpretation of the rating scale itself.

Figure 3.3 Example of a personality trait rating

Instruction to appraiser
Please circle the number on each rating scale which you feel is most
applicable to the employee.

1. How confident is the employee?

    1   2   3   (4)   5

    Low   High
    confidence   confidence

2. How much enthusiasm does the employee show in carrying
    out his/her job?

    1   2   3   4   (5)

    Unenthusiastic   Extremely
                                                   enthusiastic

3. How mature is this employee?

    1   2   3   (4)   5

    Immature   Extremely
                                                   mature

4. How steady is this employee under pressure?

    1   2   (3)   4   5

    Unstable   Highly
                                                   stable

Source: Anderson (1986)

Figure 3.4   Example of a graphic rating scale

Instruction to appraiser
Please place a tick somewhere on the line running from 'very high' to
'very low' to indicate the employee's performance for each quality.

Quality	Scale	
Quantity of work	✓	
Consider the amount of work accomplished.	very high output	very low output
Quality of work	✓	
Consider the accuracy of work and the extent to which work of a high standard is regularly produced.	very high quality of work	very low quality of work
Co-operation with others	✓	
Consider level of co-operation shown at work towards peers.	very high co-operation	very low co-operation
Innovation	✓	
Consider the extent to which suggestions for carrying out work in a new but better way are made.	very high innovation	very low innovation

Source: Anderson (1986)

Figure 3.5   Example of a forced distribution method outline

Instruction to appraiser
On any one quality, about 40% of the employees rated by you should be
rated in the middle category; around 20% of your employees in each of
categories 2 and 4, and around 10% in each of categories 1 and 5.

A.   Quality of work

10%	20%	40%	20%	10%
☐	☐	☐	☐	☐
low	below average	average	above average	high

B.   Attitude to work (enthusiasm; willingness to accept instructions)

10%	20%	40%	20%	10%
☐	☐	☐	☐	☐
low	below average	average	above average	high

C.   Flexibility (ability to adapt easily to change)

10%	20%	40%	20%	10%
☐	☐	☐	☐	☐
low	below average	average	above average	high

Source: Anderson (1986)

Forced distribution

A number of categories are established for each work quality that
is to be assessed (see figure 3.5): low, below average, average,
above average, high.

The distinguishing characteristic of this method is that a prede-
termined percentage of the group of employees to be assessed must
be placed in each category. The assumption underlying this method
is that variations in employee performance follow a normal distribution curve. Thus, in practical terms, the appraiser may be required
to assign:

Figure 3.6 Normal distribution curve (shown for employee performance)

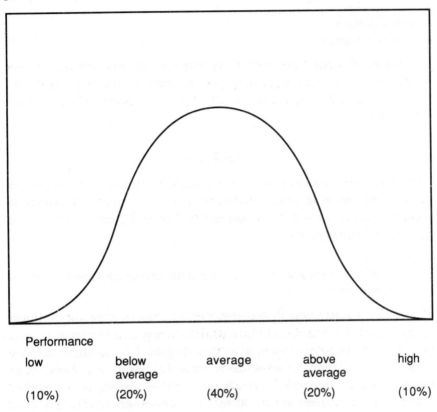

Performance				
low	below average	average	above average	high
(10%)	(20%)	(40%)	(20%)	(10%)

Source: Anderson (1986)

- 10 per cent of employees to the lowest performance category
- 20 per cent to the next category
- the largest number, say 40 per cent, to the middle category
- 20 per cent to the next
- 10 per cent to the highest category.

This approximates to the normal distribution curve shown in figure 3.6.

Although figure 3.5 shows the application of the forced distribution approach to several job elements, it can also be applied to the assessment of overall performance. To be realistic, however, this method requires a large number of employees in order to place a significant number in each of the five categories.

However, this method has the advantages of reducing the problems of:

- over-leniency
- over-strictness
- central tendency.

The major disadvantage is that variations in the performance levels of the group of employees may not conform to the normal distribution curve and so appraisers will be forced to incorrectly categorize some appraisees.

Ranking

This is the simplest performance appraisal method. The appraiser places employees in order of merit (best to poorest). Ranking is usually carried out on an assessment of overall performance. The obvious advantages are:

- simplicity
- it forces the appraiser to discriminate between different levels of performance.

The major limitation is that a group of employees may not conform to the distribution dictated by straight ranking. For instance all may be below or above average performers. Figure 3.7 assumes no more than eight employees have to be ranked. For larger numbers, extra rows would be needed on the form. This approach is sometimes referred to as 'attention ranking': the appraiser selects the best performer, then the worst, then the next best, followed by the next worst, and so on, until the whole group of employees is ranked. This permits appraisers to start by identifying extremes of performance, before undertaking the often more difficult task of discriminating among the middle performers.

Paired comparisons

This is a form of ranking in which the appraiser is required to indicate which of two employees is rated higher, in a series of pairs (figure 3.8). The number of times each individual is preferred is calculated, and a performance rating index determined, based on the number of times an employee is rated higher than his/her peers.

For example, in a group of seven employees, each employee would be compared with each of the other six. If Smith is ranked

Figure 3.7   Example of a ranking method outline

Instruction to appraiser
- List in any order, in the space below, all employees whom you are responsible for appraising.
- Look over the list and decide who you feel has been the best performer over the past year, draw a line through his/her name and write it in the space marked '1 – Highest'.
- Look over the remaining names and decide who has been the poorest performer, draw a line through his/her name and write it in the space marked '1 – Lowest'.
- Next, select the person you think is the second best performer, draw a line through his/her name and write it in the space marked '2 – Highest'.
- Select the person who has performed least well of those remaining on the list, draw a line through his/her name and write it in the space marked '2 – Lowest'.
- Continue this ranking procedure, selecting next highest, then next lowest, until you have drawn a line through every name on the list.

Employees to be ranked	Rankings	
(List names in any order in this column)	1 – highest	(insert name)
	2 – next highest	
	3 – next highest	
	4 – next highest	
	4 – next lowest	
	3 – next lowest	
	2 – next lowest	
	1 – lowest	

Source: Anderson (1986)

Figure 3.8   Example of a paired comparisons method

Instruction to appraiser
In each row compare each pair of names, i.e. the employee A. Smith
and each other employee in the same work group; indicate 'higher' if
you rank Smith's performance better during the past year, and 'lower' if
you consider it lower.

Name of employee	Other employees in the same work group	Overall work performance Higher/Lower
A. Smith	B. White	Higher
A. Smith	C. Brown	Higher
A. Smith	D. Black	Lower
A. Smith	etc.	etc.
A. Smith	etc.	etc.

Source: Anderson (1986)

higher than five, but lower than one, his performance index, using
the paired comparison approach, would be 5/6 = 0.83. If Brown is
ranked higher than two of her colleagues and lower than 4, her
index would be 2/6 = 0.33. An index of 1 is the highest obtainable,
and would be gained by an employee ranked higher than all his or
her peers. A score of 0 would be gained by someone ranked lower
than all his or her peers. Employees are placed in rank order according to their performance index scores: the higher the score the
better the performance level.

A paired comparison approach, more complex than this example,
could be devised to compare employees on a range of job dimensions, as well as an overall job performance.

The method forces appraisers to consider the relative strengths
and weaknesses of employees. It does not, however, make for easy
comparison of performance levels between groups and is unlikely
to provide employees with useful feedback that will help them

improve their future performance. Further, appraisers may be reluctant to make comparisons of this type among their staff.

This approach becomes very complex and time-consuming if large numbers of employees have to be assessed. For example, twenty-one comparisons are required to rank just seven employees and sixty-six comparisons are needed if the number of employees rises to twelve!

Assessing the Methods

The advantages and disadvantages of the seven methods of performance appraisal that we have just examined are summarized in table 3.1. They have fallen out of favour for several reasons:

- The difficulty of communicating to employees the results of such methods.
- Many managers dislike 'playing God' by appraising their staff on the basis of subjective characteristics which are not at all easy to measure.
- The results of subjective assessments, if negative, are often resented and resisted by staff which, of course, tends to destroy the whole point of the exercise.

So far seven appraisal methods have been described, with their advantages and disadvantages identified. Although these methods have fallen to some extent out of favour, you will still find them, or elements of them, used in some organizations. Contemporary performance appraisal concentrates on the more objective assessment of an employee's performance, while recognizing that subjectivity can only be minimized, never eliminated.

Appraisal Methods that Assess an Employee's Performance

A further six appraisal methods are now described and evaluated. These methods emphasize to a greater extent an employee's job performance rather than his or her personality.

These six further methods of performance appraisal involve a more objective form of evaluation and emphasize what an employee actually does and how well he or she does it.

Table 3.1 Comparison of subjective appraisal methods

Methods	Advantages	Disadvantages
Alphabetical/numerical rating	• Easily understood • Easy to use	• Rater bias • Central tendency
Forced choice rating	• Easily understood • Easy to use • Reduces the problems of central tendency, over-leniency, over-strictness	• Difficult to standardize performance indicators • Large amount of development work required for design and analysis
Personality trait rating	• Easily understood • Easy to use	• Difficult to agree a common meaning of the characteristics being assessed • Appraiser reluctance to assess employees' personalities • Appraisee resentment and rejection of personality criticisms
Graphic rating scale	• Easily understood • Easy to use • Avoids placing people in specific categories ('good', 'poor' etc.)	• Rater bias • Central tendency • Meaning or interpretation of the rating scale itself
Forced distribution	• Avoids problems of central tendency, over-leniency and over-strictness	• Group performance may not fit the pattern of the normal distribution curve • Unrealistic if too few employees
Ranking	• Simple to use • Forces appraiser to discriminate between different levels of performance	• Group may not conform to a distribution dictated by a straight-ranking (e.g. all employees may be below or above average performers)
Paired comparisons	• Forces appraisers to compare relative strengths and weaknesses of employees	• Does not allow easy comparison between different groups of workers • No clear feedback to employees to improve future performance • Appraisers may be reluctant to make employee comparisons

Source: Anderson (1986)

The six methods are:

- Free-written report.
- Controlled written report.
- Critical incidents technique.
- Results-oriented schemes.
- Self-appraisal.
- Behaviourally anchored rating scales.

Free-written report

The appraiser is given the opportunity to write an account of the performance of each of the employees that report to him or her in an unstructured form. This corresponds to what Locher and Teel (1977) describe as the 'essay method'.

A typical invitation to prepare a free-written report is:

> What is your evaluation of this employee's performance over the review period? Indicate the criteria you feel are appropriate to assess performance. You should comment both on past performance and on future changes/improvements/new targets required. You are free to write as long an essay as you wish about the employee's performance.

The chief strength of this approach is that it forces the appraiser to give careful thought to employees' performance and can produce useful comments relating both to their current performance and their potential. However, it may be difficult to compare one person with another.

Controlled written report

This method is similar to the free-written method, but uses headings in the documentation to guide the appraiser's comments. This helps to cross-compare employees.

Like the free-written report, this method also forces the appraiser to give careful thought to employees' performance and can produce useful comments relating both to their current performance and future potential. In addition, the headings used to guide the appraiser's comments will assist comparison among employees (see figure 3.9).

Figure 3.9   Example of a controlled written report outline

Instruction to appraiser You may add items or delete them as you wish.	
Technical effectiveness	*Comments/observations of appraiser*
• technical breadth and versatility • technical problem-solving and decision-making • awareness of recent developments	
Cost effectiveness	*Comments/observations of appraiser*
• direct contribution to cost reduction efforts • awareness of importance of cost factors	
Position effectiveness	*Comments/observations of appraiser*
• effectiveness of speech and writing • effectiveness in establishing rapport and securing support • regard for company objectives	

Source: Anderson (1986)

Figure 3.10 Example of a completed critical incidents method form

Positive performance		Ineffective performance
Maintained productivity levels despite batches of poor raw materials	*Productivity*	
Recommended a new method of work organization Later successfully implemented	*Innovation*	
Good oral presentation to new suppliers on technical requirements	*Communications*	Produced report containing excessive technical jargon, not easily understood by finance/marketing

Instruction to appraiser
For each of the categories shown, please record on a weekly basis for each employee:

- positive instances of job performance (on the left-hand side)
- the instances of ineffective performance (on the right-hand side).

Source: Anderson (1986)

Critical incidents technique

This method is a variant of the free-written report method. Its distinctive feature is that the appraiser is asked to record what he or she perceives as critical incidents in each employee's performance over the review period. Thus the basis for written evaluation is factually documented (see figure 3.10).

Some entries will highlight effective performance, others will point out problems or ineffective performance, thus creating an overall picture of the individual's performance. The appraiser is forced to think carefully about the performance of each employee weekly and make specific comments about particular incidents. This information should be used to provide useful feedback for bringing about future performance improvement.

There is a danger, however, that overemphasizing a small number of specific incidents during each week relating to performance, whether good or bad, may lead to a distorted view of an employee's performance over the whole time period that is being reviewed. Further, there is the danger that it can encourage extremely close supervision, with employees feeling that everything they do is being recorded.

Results-oriented schemes

These schemes do not necessarily imply the existence of a management by objectives (MBO) scheme, but usually originate from an MBO type of scheme. The appraiser is required to rate employees against previously agreed objectives or key results areas. Advocates of this method stress the importance of ensuring that both appraiser and employee participate in the objective-setting process, leading to mutually agreed objectives against which the employee's subsequent performance can be assessed. Figure 3.11 illustrates the kind of documentation that is often associated with the results-oriented method.

One of the limitations of this approach is that an employee may fail to achieve objectives through no fault of his or her own because of a change in the business environment (for example, a shift in market demand, dearer raw materials, labour disputes, changes in government economic policy). Another potential problem is that the appraiser may focus exclusively on results without paying due attention to the means by which the results were achieved.

The arguments in its favour are that:

- It emphasizes performance rather than personality factors.
- It is less likely to be influenced by the subjective viewpoint of the appraiser.

Finally, the results-oriented approach will provide a sound mechanism for providing feedback and encouraging appraiser and

Figure 3.11 Example of a results-oriented scheme outline

Instruction to appraiser
Complete appraisal documents for each of your subordinates.

[Note: The categories represented below would normally occupy several pages in an appraisal document.]

Quantitative Goals		
Describe goals	Describe results achieved	Describe reasons for difference

Qualitative Goals		
Describe goals	Describe results achieved	Describe reasons for difference

Other Contributions

Overall comments by appraiser

Signed . . . .   Date . . . .

Overall comments by head of dept/director

Signed . . . .   Date . . . .

Comments by appraisee

Signed . . . .   Date . . . .

Source: Anderson (1986)

employee to discuss openly ways of improving and developing performance to higher levels.

Self-appraisal

With this method the employee is given the opportunity to comment on his or her own performance in the appraisal documents, and to put forward suggestions relating to, for example, the modification of the job description and further training and development (see figure 3.12). It should be emphasized, however, that this approach is usually seen as an addition to the appraiser's task of evaluating the employee, using one or more of the methods listed above. Because of its importance self-appraisal is discussed in depth in a later chapter (chapter 7).

This approach deliberately seeks to involve the employee in the appraisal process and encourages him or her to prepare for the appraisal interview and to think carefully about work problems and performance. It does, however, have the difficulty of persuading an employee to produce a self-appraisal report which in some organizations becomes a permanent record.

Behaviourally anchored rating scales

Another important method, referred to as 'behaviourally anchored rating scales' (BARS) has emerged in recent years, particularly in the USA. This method, although not yet widely used, appears to have considerable advantages in overcoming some of the problems that are likely to characterize conventional alphabetical/numerical rating scales (see figure 3.13).

BARS requires a specially designed rating form for each group of jobs. The first step is to identify the key job dimensions or areas of responsibility for each job, or group of related jobs. A scale is then devised for each dimension, with a number of points from 'excellent' or 'very good' to 'unacceptable' or 'very poor'. A short statement is then inserted against each of the scale values. In this way the scale values are said to be 'anchored'. These statements are intended to indicate typical employee behaviour for the particular scale value to which they are attached.

Advantages and disadvantages

Table 3.2 summarizes the advantages and disadvantages of the six appraisal methods described above.

Figure 3.12 Example of a self-appraisal review form

Instruction
This form is issued to you for completion to help promote and guide a discussion between you and your manager about your job performance during the past 12 months. The purpose of the discussion is to help you establish guidelines to improve your performance and agree steps for your development and training. The discussion should result in a clearer understanding of:

- the main purpose of your job, its scope and the main activities required for its accomplishment;
- the critical targets and tasks which are agreed by you both as necessary and achievable;
- the means by which you can determine your success in carrying out the agreed plans and the signalling of any obstacles.

Do you have a complete understanding of the requirements of your job? If 'no', specify the areas which are not clear.

What have you accomplished during the period under review?

Are there any changes you think could help you accomplish more in the forthcoming period?

What parts of your job do you do best?	What parts of your job do you do worst?

Have you any skills, aptitudes or knowledge not fully used in your job? If 'yes', what are they?

What training would help improve your performance in your job?

Signed . . . . Date . . . .

Source: Anderson (1986)

Figure 3.13   Example of a behaviourally anchored rating scale

Instruction to appraiser
Please complete appraisal documents for each of your subordinates.

JOB: Bank Teller	
Job dimension	*Client relations*
Acknowledges the presence of regular customers by recalling their names from memory.	1
Acknowledges the customer by an expression of 'thank you' or similar comment on completion of transaction.	2
Apologizes to the customer if there has been a delay in providing service.	3
Makes small talk with the customer during transaction.	4
Displays irritation if the customer has not completed forms correctly.	5
Fails to give customer correct receipts on completion of transaction.	6
Keeps customers waiting while chatting to fellow employees.	7

1 – extremely good performance
2 – good performance
3 – slightly good performance
4 – neither good nor bad performance
5 – slightly poor performance
6 – poor performance
7 – extremely poor performance

Source: Anderson (1986)

Table 3.2 Advantages and disadvantages of objective methods

Methods	Advantages	Disadvantages
Free written report	• Forces the appraiser to think carefully about an employee • Can produce useful comment on both current performance and future potential	• Comparison among individuals may be difficult
Controlled written report	• Forces appraiser to think carefully about an employee • Can produce useful comment on both current performance and potential performance • Headings can help cross-comparisons among employees	• Makes comparisons among individuals difficult
Critical incident technique	• Appraiser is forced to think carefully about each employee • Provides useful feedback for future improvement	• Overemphasis on a small number of specific events leads to a distorted view of an employee's overall performance • May encourage excessively close supervision and employee resentment and demotivation
Results-oriented schemes	• Emphasize performance rather than personality • Is less likely to be influenced by the subjective viewpoint of the appraiser • Encourages open discussion in formulating objectives • Provides feedback for future improvement	• Appraiser may be unaware that the employee's failure to achieve objectives was due to external factors and not the employee's inadequate performance • Danger of focusing solely on results and ignoring the means used to achieve results
Self-appraisal	• Involves employee in the appraisal process • Encourages employee to prepare for the appraisal interview and to think carefully about work problems and performance	• The difficulty of persuading an employee to produce a self-appraisal report which may become a permanent record
Behaviourally anchored rating scales	• Provides useful feedback to employees	• Expensive to develop

Source: Anderson (1986)

Selecting an Appropriate Appraisal Method

The choice of an appropriate method depends on a number of factors:

(a)   *Performance appraisal objectives*   The objectives and philosophy of the performance appraisal scheme should be the major determining influence in the method chosen.

(b)   *The nature of the organization structure*   The extent to which the organization structure is flat or hierarchical will influence the closeness of the relationships, and frequency of interactions between manager and employees. This in turn may impact upon what method of appraisal is selected.

(c)   *Levels and types of staff*   Organizations that introduce performance appraisal schemes to cover all levels of employees must consider the question of design variants, in selecting the most suitable appraisal method for different groups of staff. For example, Long (1986) identifies that results-oriented schemes tend to be primarily used in appraising managers, while personality-oriented or behavioural rating scales are predominately used for non-managerial staff.

Familiarity with Performance Appraisal

How familiar an organization and its staff are with performance appraisal will influence the decisions on which appraisal method to adopt. There is some evidence that when first adopting performance appraisal organizations often opt for more structured approaches (e.g. rating scales), and later move to less structured approaches as appraisers become more familiar with the philosophy, objectives and priorities of performance appraisal.

Long (1986) draws attention to a trend where more organizations are adopting composite approaches, consisting of an amalgamation of methods, as a way of combating the limitations of particular methods, and reflecting the multiple purposes and considerations that must be taken into account.

References

Anderson, G.C. 1986: *Performance Appraisal*. Strathclyde: University of Strathclyde Business School/HMSO.

Locher, A.H. and Tell, K.S. 1977: Performance Appraisal: A Survey of Current Practices. *Personnel Journal*, 56 (5), May.

Long, P. 1986: *Performance Appraisal Revisited*. London: IPM.

4

Sources of Performance Appraisal

Who takes responsibility for undertaking the appraisal of staff is a key decision in the design of any system of performance appraisal. Also of great importance are the sources of information about the performance of staff that individuals designated as having responsibility for appraising particular employees can access.

Who Conducts the Appraisal Interview?

Most of the research evidence suggests the commonest practice is for the task of appraisal interview to be undertaken by the immediate line manager. In a national study of UK performance appraisal practices Gill (1977) reports that, for the responding organizations:

- 86 per cent of appraisal interviews are carried out by the employee's immediate line manager.
- 7 per cent are by the immediate line manager's manager (i.e. by the 'grandfather' or 'grandmother' figure).
- One per cent is by some kind of committee arrangement involving more than one person.

A later survey carried out by Long (1986) shows even greater emphasis on the immediate line manager, shown to be the appraiser in 98 per cent of the organizations covered by the survey.

Similar research findings emerge from the USA. The great majority of organizations there have adopted the view that the immediate line manager of the employee being appraised should write appraisal reports and conduct appraisal interviews. The essential argument in support of this practice is that these tasks are an integral part of the management process and that the immediate line manager, through close working contact and through guiding and controlling employees' activities, is in a better position than anyone else in the organization to evaluate employees' performance, strengths and weaknesses, and training and development needs relating to the current job.

In considering design and implementation issues elsewhere in the book, the assumption is generally made that organizations are operating conventional systems, with the immediate line manager in the role as appraiser. In this chapter some alternative approaches are considered which currently are rarely practised, or else are practised in only a small number of organizations. It is possible that some of the alternative approaches described below will become more widely used, as organizations become more aware of their benefits. Each of the alternatives has costs and difficulties that have to be weighed carefully against possible benefits.

Reviewers

One of the deficiencies of conventional performance appraisal is overemphasis on a single rater, who is usually the immediate line manager. Another possible difficulty, though one which can be overcome, concerns the motivation and skills of the immediate line managers as appraisers. Sashkin (1981) suggests that an important condition for effective performance appraisal is to ensure that rewards are built into the performance appraisal system, to encourage managers to carry out their appraisal duties in careful and conscientious fashion.

Many conventional appraisal systems include a review mechanism, often requiring the appraiser's manager to occupy the reviewing role. This can involve the reviewer in scrutinizing and signing-off completed appraisal forms, as a check on the consistency and fairness of appraisers. Some organizations formally extend the role of the reviewer, by encouraging or requiring appraisers to consult with reviewers prior to the appraisal interview, to ensure that any differences in the perceptions and views of appraiser and reviewer regarding the employee about to be appraised are resolved prior to the appraisal interview. In addition, where reviewers hold meetings afterwards with appraisers to discuss the evaluations of particular employees, issues relating to bias and inconsistencies can be addressed, with a view to reducing these problems in future cycles of the system of performance appraisal. Through being involved in this process reviewers, who in many systems are the appraisers of the immediate line managers, will be well placed to gather data on how effective these managers have been as appraisers. This can then become one of the criteria to be considered at their next appraisal interviews, thus giving them an incentive to take their duties as appraisers seriously.

Multi-appraisal

While the use of reviewers removes some of the problems of a single-rater approach, other organizations have moved towards more ambitious multi-appraisal systems. Stinson and Stokes (1980) describe a pioneering study in the use of multi-appraisal in Gulf Oil, where a system was devised to cope with around thirty senior managers operating in North Sea locations. To overcome the limitations not only of the single-rater approach but also of the fact that immediate line managers were often geographically far away, located, for example, in North or South America, the decision was made to focus on the job network as the relevant group for performance appraisal, while retaining some elements of conventional performance appraisal. The job network was defined as those key people in the organization on whom the performance of the individual being assessed principally impacts. The members of the job network can be peers, subordinates or others at a more senior level, but in the Gulf Oil example it excluded the immediate line manager.

In Gulf Oil, the steps involved in the multi-appraisal system are outlined below:

1. Managers who are to be appraised under this scheme are asked to identify the members of their job network who will subsequently become involved in their appraisal. The company established parameters of not less than five, and not more than eight members of anyone's job network.
2. The members of the job network are issued with a rating-scale document by the company's Human Resource Department, asking them to complete a set of ratings scales assessing different aspects of the performance (over a twelve-month time period) of the person being appraised. These completed documents are returned directly to the Human Resource Department.

3. The Human Resource Department then collate a summary of the ratings, copies of the summary document being distributed to the appraisee, and to the appraisee's line manager, who up till now has not been involved in the process. The anonymity of the members of the job network is preserved. Neither appraisee nor appraisee's line manager can relate elements of the summary feedback sheet to any particular member of the job network.
4. The appraisee is next invited to complete a self-assessment document, a copy of which is passed to the appraisee's line manager.
5. The appraisee's immediate line manager now conducts an appraisal interview with the individual concerned. The line manager's preparations are aided both by the summary feedback document from the members of the job network, and by the self-assessment document completed by the appraisee.
6. The line manager completes the company's official appraisal document.

Positive results were reported on implementation of this scheme. The multi-rater approach generated data of a highly specific nature, with many practical comments and suggestions as to where and how performance could be improved. Another important benefit of multi-appraisal was the identification of key organizational weaknesses, as well as evaluations of individuals. The multi-assessment approach did not appear to result in over-ratings. The final grades given by appraisers were not significantly higher than in the period prior to the introduction of the multi-appraisal scheme.

Peer Appraisal

Although research evidence relating to the reliability and validity of appraisals carried out by co-workers or peers is generally positive, few organizations have actually introduced peer appraisals. Although Thompson (1991) cites cases where American organizations (e.g. Quaker Oats and W.L. Gore & Associates) have been using peer-based performance appraisals for many years, Kane and Lawler (1978) have put forward a range of explanations as to why relatively little progress has been made in designing systems of performance appraisal based on peer review.

Their reasons include:

- The common belief that peer ratings are subject to distortion, depending on the popularity of individuals.
- The failure of many managers to recognize benefits in seeking inputs

from the appraisee's peers. Additional reasons for the low use of performance appraisal by peers put forward by Smith (1976) and by DeNisi and Mitchell (1978) include:

- Managers feel threatened by the idea of relinquishing control to employees.
- Friendship ratings.
- Subgroup bias (e.g. tendency of members of any subgroup or informal group to give high ratings to other members of the group).
- Reliance of peers on stereotypes, in making evaluations.
- Possibility of future retaliation, if ratings are received from co-workers that are felt to be unfairly low.

There is, however, a case that can be made for the use of peer appraisal. Williams and Herriot (1989) point out that using peers introduces a perspective different from that of line managers, and makes it possible to obtain a number of independent judgements. Williams and Herriot suggest that the average of these may be superior to any single judgement. Latham and Wexley (1981) conclude that two factors – the number of independent judgements and the extent to which employees interact with peers – help to explain the acceptable standards of reliability of peer appraisal that has emerged in a number of studies.

The extent to which employees interact, and so are in a position to take an informal view on the performance of colleagues, and their willingness to act as appraisers of colleagues are two crucial issues that must be addressed in considering whether to introduce a peer system of performance appraisal. This later point is emphasized by Thompson (1991) who stresses that a genuinely participative corporate culture, with a non-hierarchical team-based organizational philosophy, is a necessary condition for the effective use of peer appraisal. If organizational structures become flatter and less hierarchical along the lines predicted by Handy (1989) and Kanter (1989) to cope with the increasing speed of change, it follows that wider spans of control will make it more difficult for line managers to appraise their staff. Where a line manager has, say, between five and twelve direct reports, undertaking performance appraisals is manageable although time-consuming. Dealing with thirty or forty direct reports would mean that an increasing number of organizations would have to reassess the design of their systems of performance appraisal if the demands on line managers become too onerous. The greater use of peer appraisal is one option that may well become increasingly utilized.

The possible introduction of peer appraisal needs, however, to be approached with caution. In a study of user acceptance of an existing peer appraisal system, which had been operating for six years, Cederblom and Lounsbury (1980) reported a relatively low acceptance of peer evaluations in a survey of 174 participants in a scheme in an academic institution. McEvoy and Buller (1987) found more favourable attitudes in a study of peer appraisal in an industrial company. Of the 218 respondents, while 16 per cent favoured outright elimination of peer review, only 17 per cent favoured continuation of the scheme without change. The majority (67 per cent) favoured continuation of the concept provided some revisions were made. Respondents in the survey were generally more favourably disposed to the use of peers as appraisers for developmental purposes than they were to their use for evaluative purposes. The respondents stressed the importance of maintaining the confidentiality of peer ratings provided. This emerged as an important consideration in designing a performance appraisal system using peers as raters. The anonymity principle used by Gulf Oil in the illustration of a multi-appraiser approach seems equally applicable in a peer rating system.

Subordinate Appraisal

This approach refers to situations where organizations operate systems of performance appraisal which give employees a formal opportunity to make an assessment of the person to whom they report in the organization, as one element in the system.

This approach could be incorporated in the multi-appraiser approach previously described, where one or more direct subordinates could be part of the five to eight individuals comprising the job network, which assesses a range of aspects of a manager's performance.

Mohrman, Resnick-West and Lawler (1989) are of the opinion that ratings by subordinates can be important and valid, both because a number of people are involved in providing inputs, and because of the unique perspective of the subordinate. Williams and Herriot (1989) indicate that subordinates are well placed to make judgements about their line manager's performance on several dimensions of behaviour, but especially at managing people.

Although few examples exist where organizations make formal use of subordinates' assessments in their systems of performance appraisal, some case studies report successful applications of this approach. Latham and Wexley (1981) report several American examples, in companies such as Exxon and Weyerhaeuser, where anonymous subordinate ratings have been used as an element of performance appraisal. Latham and Wexley identify benefits that can emerge from subordinate appraisal. For example, subordinates begin to see problems through the eyes of their manager, and the manager being appraised is made aware of issues relating to his or her performance from the perspective of subordinates. Many of the problems identified as relating to peer appraisal apply also to subordinate appraisal. Since some subordinates may feel reluctant to become involved in making assessments and many perceive the process as threatening, the principle of anonymity is important for increasing the likelihood of accurate ratings. Latham and Wexley suggest that subordinate ratings should be avoided in cases where there are few subordinates (e.g. less than four).

As in the case of peer appraisal, subordinate appraisal, although little used, may have a more important role in future. Bernardin and Beatty (1987), in outlining conditions for the use of subordinate appraisal, stress the importance of a participative climate to increase the likelihood of success.

Appraisal by External Parties

It is possible to make use of people from outside the immediate work environment to undertake performance appraisals. These could cover a range of sources, for example personnel specialists, clients and customers, trained independent observers, assessors in assessment centres. The topic of assessment centres is dealt with in chapter 10, since assessment centres complement rather than replace systems of performance appraisal, and are normally concerned with the evaluation of employee potential rather than current performance. The other parties mentioned can all provide useful inputs to the performance appraisal process, but are unlikely to prove satisfactory in conducting performance appraisals. All external parties suffer the disadvantage that they do not know, at first hand, the relevant background to performance issues in terms of discussions between line managers and their staffs. In addition, inefficiencies are likely to be associated with appraisals conducted by external parties in that more time and manpower is likely to be used.

Self-appraisal

Self-appraisal, in the sense of encouraging the appraisee to make an active contribution to the appraisal process, is a topic of great importance, and many systems of performance appraisal have been designed to include this aspect. This topic merits in-depth treatment and is the subject of chapter 7.

Summary

The assumption throughout this book is that the usual practice in most systems of performance appraisal is for the immediate line manager of the appraisee to be the appraiser. An increasingly common practice, as noted in this chapter, is for the immediate line manager's manager to have an active role, as a reviewer.

This chapter explored alternative sources – multi-appraisal, peer appraisal, subordinate appraisal, appraisal by external parties and self-appraisal (discussed in chapter 7). I agree with the view of Latham and Wexley (1981) that while it is sound practice for immediate line managers to be appraisers, the use of multiple approaches – used in addition to, and not as a replacement for, the immediate line manager – increases the probability of obtaining a comprehensive and accurate picture of an employee's total performance contribution to the organization. Since employees may behave differently with managers, peers and subordinates, a range of inputs from these different sources should prove useful, provided a participative, non-threatening corporate culture has been established. Self-appraisal, as discussed later, certainly can play a useful role. I remain sceptical about involving external parties.

References

Bernardin, H.J. and Beatty, R.W. 1987: Can subordinate appraisals enhance managerial productivity? *Sloan Management Review*, 28 (4).

Cederblom, D. and Lounsbury, J.W. 1980: An investigation of user acceptance of peer evaluation. *Personnel Psychology*, 33.

DeNisi, A.S. and Mitchell, J.L. 1978: An analysis of peer ratings as predictors and criterion measures and a proposed new application. *Academy of Management Review*, 3.

Gill, D. 1977: *Appraising Performance: Present Trends and the Next Decade.* London: IPM.

Handy, C. 1989: *The Age of Unreason.* London: Business Books.

Kane, J.S. and Lawler, E.E. 1978: Methods of peer assessment. *Psychological Bulletin,* 85.

Kanter, R.M. 1989: *When Giants Learn to Dance.* London: Simon & Schuster.

Latham, G.P. and Wexley, K.N. 1981: *Increasing Productivity Through Performance Appraisal.* Reading, Mass.: Addison-Wesley.

Long, P. 1986: *Performance Appraisal Revisited.* London: IPM.

McEvoy, G.M. and Buller, P.F. 1987: User acceptance of peer ratings in an industrial setting. *Personnel Psychology,* 40.

Mohrman, A.M., Resnick-West, S.M. and Lawler, E.E. 1989: *Designing Performance Appraisal Systems.* San Francisco: Jossey-Bass.

Sashkin, M. 1981: Appraising appraisal: Ten lessons from research for practice. *Organisational Dynamics,* Winter.

Smith, P.C. 1976: Behaviours, results and organisational effectiveness. In M.D. Dunnette, (ed.), *Handbook of Industrial and Organisational Psychology* 2nd edn. Chicago: Rand-McNally.

Stinson, J. and Stokes, J. 1980: How to multi-appraise. *Management Today,* June.

Thompson, B.L. 1991: An early review of peer review. *Training,* 28 (7), July.

Williams, R.S. and Herriot, P. 1989: Alternative raters and methods. In P. Herriot, (ed.), *Assessment and Selection in Organisations.* London: John Wiley.

5

Developing the Performance Appraisal System

The performance appraisal system has a key role to play in organizations in promoting positive attitudes and practices that contribute to employee effectiveness. It should also form a central element of an organization's human resource systems since, to ensure an integrated approach to HRM, it should interlock with a number of other areas of HRM including recruitment and selection, organization design, compensation, career development, training and development, and succession planning. Some of these linkages are examined in later chapters.

In designing how the system of performance appraisal should operate effectively in an organization, the emphasis should be on:

- Clarifying the objectives.
- Identifying and evaluating methods, selecting the method that best fits both the objectives set and the culture of the organization.
- Planning the elements of the performance appraisal cycle, and how they are to be linked.

Throughout the design phase, the emphasis should be on the system, and how well the various elements interact and harmonize. Mohrman, Resnick-West and Lawler (1989) identify four principal activities of the performance appraisal cycle (illustrated in figure 5.1):

1. Defining what performance is, or should be.
2. Measuring and evaluating performance.
3. Providing individuals with feedback, and an opportunity to discuss their performance, with a view to helping them to improve their performance.
4. Generating information for use by other systems in the organization.

Figure 5.1   The performance appraisal cycle

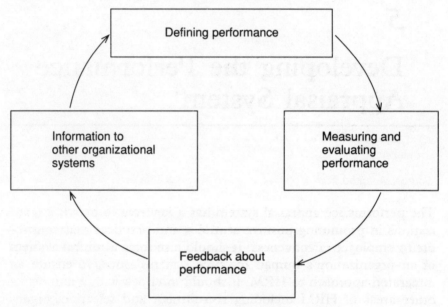

Source: Mohrman, Resnick-West & Lawler (1989)

Defining Performance

At the beginning of the performance appraisal cycle, managers and their staff should agree on what kinds of performance, and what levels of performance are required. Disagreements and acrimony in the later measurement and feedback phases can often be overcome when more effort is devoted to defining the performance that is subsequently to be evaluated (Wexley and Klimoski, 1984). According to Mohrman, Resnick-West and Lawler (1989), the assessment of performance can focus on any, or all of the fundamental components of performance, shown in figure 5.2.

While there are many different options, with regard to the choice of performance appraisal methods (as explained in detail in chapter 3), most appraisal methods fall broadly into three categories that correspond to the main components of performance encountered in any job. As shown in figure 5.2, traditional performance-appraised methods tend to focus on the characteristics of the individual performer; other methods, for example behaviourally anchored

Figure 5.2 Components of performance

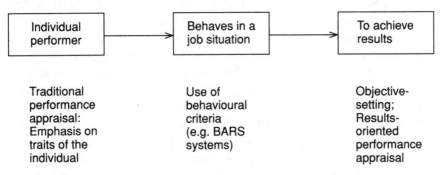

Individual performer	Behaves in a job situation	To achieve results
Traditional performance appraisal: Emphasis on traits of the individual	Use of behavioural criteria (e.g. BARS systems)	Objective-setting; Results-oriented performance appraisal

Source: Adapted from Mohrman, Resnick-West & Lawler (1989)

rating scales, lead to an assessment of employees using behavioural criteria.

Modern trends in performance appraisal focus increasingly on results or outcomes as the most satisfactory basis for appraiser and appraisee to agree and define what kind of performance and performance level is expected of them.

Objective setting

Setting and agreeing objectives as a basis for subsequent appraisal of performance is generally seen as a legitimate and appropriate way for managers to agree performance criteria with each member of their staff. There is substantial evidence nevertheless (see, for example, Evenden and Anderson, 1992) that objectives are often set in a sloppy, careless fashion that makes later appraisal against these objectives difficult. Many managers appear to lack skills in agreeing effective objectives with each of their staff in the initial stage in the performance appraisal cycle. To be effective, objectives should be:

- verifiable (in the sense that clear criteria are agreed and set)
- quantifiable (where possible)
- achievable
- challenging
- significant.

If objectives are set at a level that an individual feels is beyond the scope of his or her abilities, this is likely to be demotivating, and could have an adverse effect on performance and morale. Ideally, objectives should be set at such a level that they are challenging in the sense of stretching the individual to develop existing skills or acquire new skills to achieve their fulfilment. Objectives should be significant in the sense of being meaningful to all parties concerned. The number of objectives set and agreed – not too many (preferably between four and eight) – should be representative of the main functions of an individual's job. Job analysis is a useful first step in clarifying areas in which objectives can be set. While setting objectives is increasingly seen as the most satisfactory base for defining performance, a number of problems can readily occur.

Some of the issues most commonly reported in organizations include:

1. *Failing to make clear the criteria or measure to be used* in assessing whether the objective can be achieved or not. Failure in this respect means that no sound base has been established for subsequent appraisal. It is very likely that disagreement and acrimony will occur at the appraisal interview if appraisers and appraisees have had different, unspecified criteria in mind.
2. *Failing to make explicit critical parameters, especially timescales and constraints such as budget limits.* For the successful achievement of an objective it is usually important that it is completed by a specific date, and without spending more than a specified sum of money. If either or both of these factors is not included or made clear, the value of completion of the objective to the organization may be diminished, or even invalidated.
3. *Setting too many objectives.* Setting and agreeing too many objectives tends to dissipate the efforts of a member of staff, and fails to provide a focus on the central purpose of jobs.
4. *Setting objectives which do not fully reflect the individual's contribution.* Ideally, a small number of objectives should be set which are central to jobs. Dangers are that objectives are set primarily in new areas of activity, neglecting existing forms of work, or that they are formulated in those parts of jobs that are most readily quantified. It is important that due recognition should be placed in performance appraisal on contributions made by individuals not reflected in the objectives that have been agreed and set, but which nevertheless have an impact on the overall effectiveness of individuals.

As identified in figure 5.2, performance can also be defined in terms of job behaviour and competencies, as opposed to the results that are to be achieved. For example, in the case of a bank teller, one dimension of performance will refer to the behaviour expected in dealing with customers. This approach will harmonize with the use, noted in chapter 3, of behaviourally anchored rating scales for performance appraisal, when the individual employee receives feedback on the type of behaviour and appropriateness of behaviour that the appraiser considers has been achieved.

As indicated by several writers including, for example, Dulewicz and Fletcher (1989), techniques such as repertory grid, critical incidents or structured questionnaires have proved to be useful in identifying critical job competencies. Examples of job competencies include planning, interpersonal skills and communication skills. Each should be conveyed in such a way as to show a clear meaning, and to relate to behaviour that can be observed.

A third approach, evident from figure 5.2, is to define performance in terms of the characteristics of the performer. This is likely to prove more subjective and problematical, given the difficulty of changing individuals, and defining precise characteristics in objective terms. See chapter 3 for more detailed consideration of appraisal methods.

The process of defining performance will involve several parties. Who should be involved is a question that should be addressed when designing the performance appraisal system, although a good system will incorporate some flexibility in this respect in order to permit the views of a range of different parties to be drawn upon in defining performance requirements for individual employees. A central issue, addressed in chapter 4 concerns who should carry out appraisals. As discussed in chapter 7, however, a sound process for defining performance and performance requirements should include some input from the individuals being appraised. Joint activity in this area will contribute to employee feelings of ownership of the appraisal process and considered by, for example, Greller (1978) to be an essential ingredient for effective performance appraisal.

Measuring and Evaluating Performance

The major issues concerning the measurement and evaluation of performance relate to the question of who appraises performance, the type of measures used, when they will be made. Ideally, agreement on performance measures should be reached at the beginning of the performance appraisal cycle, when appraisers and appraisees meet to define performance requirements. The measurement process is likely to be effective when it is two-way, involving employees in accepting some responsibility for monitoring their own performance, as opposed to a purely 'top-down' situation in which the appraiser applies measures to the work of staff. Another useful ingredient is a supportive organizational climate in which employees and their managers feel at ease in exchanging views on measures, and their perceptions and interpretations of measures relating to performance, as part of the ongoing manager/employee relationship. A number of methods are available in gathering information to apply measures. These include the following.

Direct observation This approach is important since it means appraisers can obtain some information direct, without the possibility of distortion that results from gaining information from indirect sources. Its deficiencies are that it is time-consuming, and difficult to apply, for example, in a very 'flat' organization structure with few hierarchical levels where spans of control are large. In addition, an appraiser can normally hope at best to obtain a limited number of snapshots of employee performance from time to time through direct observation. A major issue is how representative and reliable the samples of information obtained through direct observation are of the total performance of employees.

Self-completion diaries Self-completion diaries undertaken by job holders may assist in providing information to appraisers about the mix of activities of employees, and their time prioritization. At best, they are likely to be kept only for a short period, as most people find this an onerous task to undertake for any great length of time – a single week is probably about the maximum.

Critical incident methods The broad philosophy of this approach, pioneered by Flanagan (1953), is to select a small number of incidents in which the performance of individuals has been particularly effective and ineffective, with as much supporting evidence as possible to provide reasons for both high effectiveness and high ineffectiveness. This approach can be used on a self-assessment basis by employees, and by managers. It can be useful in highlighting the strengths and limitations of individual employees, but suffers the disadvantage that it neglects intermediate zones of performance by focusing on extreme cases.

Repertory grid This technique has a number of uses; in terms of applying measures in performance appraisal it can be used to clarify the thinking of an appraiser along the following lines. The appraiser might sub-divide the group of employees to be assessed into those considered to be effective, and those considered to be ineffective.

The appraiser would then take two of the effective group and one of the ineffective, and attempt to specify in what way two are alike, but different from the third. For example, two might have high interpersonal skills, while the third does not. The appraiser would then be in a position to test the proposition that has been formulated, that good interpersonal skills characterize the high-performing group but are absent from the low performers. The process is then repeated with a different group of three, to identify in what way two are alike, but different from the third. In this way a list of constructs or dimensions is built up to provide a picture of factors and measures that help to explain effective and ineffective performance. The process has the added advantage of helping appraisers to develop their insights into the determinants of effective performance, and to sharpen their awareness of appropriate measure to employ in monitoring the performance of employees.

Providing Individuals with Feedback and an Opportunity to Discuss their Performance

The most obvious place where feedback is provided is in the appraisal interview, seen by many organizations as the central and most important element of the performance appraisal cycle. Its importance is explained largely because the exchange of feedback between appraiser and appraisee – normally a one-to-one interview – represents the culmination of the earlier stages concerned with defining and measuring performance, and generates decisions and actions that impact upon the individuals involved, especially the appraisee, and upon other aspects of HRM.

The appraisal interview is one of the most difficult interviews any manager is expected to undertake. Issues of extreme importance to individual employees are discussed which can have a major impact on their future. Because individuals may feel threatened or anxious in appraisal interviews, high levels of interviewing and interpersonal skills on the part of managers are required, and these are discussed in greater detail in chapter 8.

In terms of considering the logistics of designing performance appraisal systems, the role of feedback should be viewed as a central element of the communication process in which the sender (the appraiser) conveys a message to the recipient (the appraisee). In a well-managed democratic appraisal interview, feedback will not be a one-way process, but will be exchanged by both parties.

The distinctive aspects about communications in the appraisal interview is that the message frequently contains information about the appraisee. The extent to which the appraisee accepts feedback, and is prepared to use it as a basis for changing behaviour, attitudes and actions will depend on a range of factors (Greller, 1980) including:

- The credibility of the source of the feedback.
- The nature of the message being conveyed.
- The characteristics of the employee being appraised.

Trust in the source is likely to be highly critical, and will depend on the extent to which trust, honesty and openness characterize the organization culture. Mohrman, Resnick-West and Lawler (1989) point out that when the source of feedback – usually the appraiser – is perceived as controlling valuable outcomes such as salary increases, job security and promotion, the recipient is likely to respond favourably to feedback, and to make changes based on it. One of the problems in appraisal interviews is that the appraiser has a wide choice of options, in selecting areas for feedback to appraisees. Feedback should contain information that influences future behaviour. Mohrman, Resnick-West and Lawler (1989) indicate that feedback can function either directionally or motivationally. Directional feedback is concerned with making clear the behaviour and actions expected of staff. If, on the other hand, feedback provides a promise or possibility of some kind of future reward, it functions as an incentive. Feedback may serve as a reward, or punishment, in itself in providing data that accords to a varying extent with the self-image held by individual employees. Research findings (Prince and Lawler, 1986) show that individuals want this kind of information. It is particularly important if employees are expected to perceive a clear performance–reward link.

Generating Information for Use by Other Systems in the Organization

Human resource management, to be effective, requires the integration of a number of elements. A central element of HRM is the performance appraisal system because, through generating valid information on the present state of the human resources of the organization, it contributes to other areas.

Recruitment and selection

Performance appraisal data can provide a sound basis for validating selection methods and selection decisions, through identifying the various levels of performance achievement of those selected by different methods. Cameron (1981) suggests this is a neglected opportunity in many organizations.

Training

The performance appraisal system is not only concerned with the evaluation of employee performance in terms of identifying results achieved. A good appraisal system should encourage analysis into why objectives have or have not been achieved, leading to conclusions about the competencies of the individual, and clarifying areas where training and development is required. Appraisal documentation normally includes data identifying training and development needs relating to the knowledge, skills, attitudes and experiences of individual employees. In collating this data, training and development plans and strategies for the whole organization and its constituent parts can be formulated.

Career development and the evaluation of employee potential

Some performance appraisal systems incorporate objectives (as previously discussed) and documentation which produce data on a range of issues relating to the career development and future potential of the individual. The data generated typically includes:

- The individual's career objectives and aspirations.
- Past and current career moves and direction.

- An evaluation of the individual's future potential.
- Earliest date for consideration for a move.
- Mobility – any constraints.
- Development activities in support of the career plan.
- A career plan, possibly including alternative paths.

Succession planning

Closely associated with career planning and the evaluation of potential is the use of performance appraisal data to build succession plans. Succession planning is usually understood to mean the identification of particular individuals as possible or likely successors to the holders of certain jobs, usually senior, or senior and middle management positions. Gratton and Syrett (1990) point out that succession strategies will depend on the structure and culture of the organization. A typical approach, however, illustrated by Mayo (1991) is to take each present managerial post above a defined level and identify and name others, usually employed within the organization, who could succeed the present job-holder. In addition, how soon each potential successor would be ready to take over is usually recorded.

Some of this data may be included in the performance appraisal documentation, and in documentation relating to the assessment of employee potential where separate systems exist for this purpose.

Since succession planning is a separate though related activity, the kind of document illustrated in figure 5.3 will normally be completed by human resource specialists, in consultation with line managers, as a separate exercise.

Pay and reward decisions

As will be discussed in chapter 9, appraisal data is increasingly being used by organizations to make current decisions on pay and rewards, and to assist in developing future strategy in this area.

Issues in the use of appraisal data for other human resource management systems

A number of issues must be addressed during the design phase of the performance appraisal system, with respect to using appraisal data for other systems.

Figure 5.3 Succession planning outline form

Job Title:

Present Job Holder:

  Age

  Grade

  Length of time in post

  Appraisal ratings: This year   Previous years

Earliest date for a move:

Assessment of potential: Quantitative rating/comment

  This year

  Previous years

Mobility level: Any constraints on mobility of individual

Moves: Other job in the organization for which the holder of this job
has been named as a possible successor.

Job: Estimate of when this individual would be ready to move to
each of the named jobs.

Successors   Names _____   When ready _____

                      _____   _____

                      _____   _____

Clarifying objectives

The importance of formulating and agreeing clear objectives for the
performance appraisal system has been stressed at length in chapter
2. The need for this becomes particularly apparent in using appraisal
data for other purposes. Precisely what other HRM systems expect
from the performance appraisal system must be defined, otherwise

incomplete or irrelevant information can readily be accumulated in appraisal documentation.

Conflicts between appraisal objectives

Schein (1978) draws attention to several dilemmas and possible conflicts that organizations must consider. One dilemma concerns the decision on what types of data should be collected, stored, and by what methods. Should this information be shared freely with the employees being appraised? Schein suggests that openness, e.g. relating to divulging ratings of future potential, may make these ratings less valid because appraisers do not want to be seen to be making judgements that could be perceived as harmful to the careers of their staff. He also draws attention to a wider dilemma, suggesting that the dominant purpose of many performance appraisal systems – to stimulate open communication between appraiser and appraisee in order to develop the appraisee's performance – may be undermined in various ways through the collection of appraisal data about individuals that is designed to be stored in central files.

Retention of appraisal data

Decisions must be made on:

• How long appraisal reports will be kept.
• Who will have access to them, and for what purpose.
• What data will be extracted from appraisal forms and stored in central files.

Some organizations do not give managers access to previous appraisals, or to appraisals carried out by their predecessors, to avoid continuing and perpetuating biases about particular individuals. On balance, however, the opposite argument tends to prevail, justifiably, on the grounds that appraisal documents can provide helpful continuity in the management of people, and that individuals are not subject to an abrupt, and possibly alarming, change in their appraisals whenever they find themselves working for a new manager.

The length of time for retaining appraisal documents on file is often determined by practical as well as business, and HRM decisions. Five to ten years is commonplace. It is possible to find archive material in organizations that extends back thirty or forty years.

Other issues on which decisions need to be taken in designing a system of performance appraisal include the following.

Number and type of employees to be included

Gill (1977) and Long (1986) highlight from survey evidence in the UK that while traditionally performance appraisal has been restricted to supervisory and managerial staff, increasingly organizations have been extending performance appraisal to cover other levels.

The reasons for this trend and its implication have been discussed in chapter 1. An important design consideration is whether the organization requires two or more design variants of its performance appraisal system, to meet the different needs of different groups of employees. Many organizations, for example, have developed a system for managerial employees, and a separate system for non-managerial employees. The arguments for developing more that one variant centre around:

- criteria for measuring and assessing performance
- levels of discretion in job
- frequency and nature of contact with managers
- educational levels of employees
- ability levels
- age ranges
- geographical locations
- functional specialisms.

For example, when an organization justifies a separate system for its managers from its non-managerial employees, the reasoning could be along the following lines. Since managers have more discretion over their work, objective-setting appraisal methods may be appropriate for them, but behavioural rating scales may be more appropriate for non-managerial employees. Because some groups of non-managerial employees may have low educational qualifications, they may not be required to complete a self-assessment whereas managers are expected to.

The Length of the Performance Appraisal Cycle

Since effective performance appraisal systems are those tailored to the organization's requirements, the length of the cycle should

harmonize with work cycles in the organization. One year is probably the commonest time interval between appraisals, though in
some cases it is shorter (six months, or even three months) and in
others (e.g. school-teachers and university lecturers) often longer,
around two years.

Timings

Various choices are available, e.g. whether to use anniversary dates,
or a fixed time period in the year; whether to appraise all employees
at the same time of year or devise a pattern of staggered timings for
different sections, departments or divisions. Increasingly, especially
as organizations develop stronger links between appraisal and pay,
the common practice is to undertake appraisals at a particular point
in the year, even if spread over a period of several weeks, often
determined by the timing of the financial year, and the budgeting
and financial planning process.

References

Cameron, D. 1981: Performance appraisal and review, *Management Decision*, 19 (6).

Dulewicz, V. and Fletcher, C.A. 1989: The context and dynamics of performance appraisal. In P. Herriot (ed.), *Assessment and Selection in Organisations*. London: John Wiley.

Evenden, R. and Anderson, G.C. 1992: *Management Skills: Making the Most of People*. Wokingham: Addison Wesley.

Flanagan, J.C. 1953: The critical incident technique, *Psychological Bulletin*, 51 (4), July.

Gill, D. 1977: *Appraising Performance*. London: IPM.

Gratton, L. and Syrett, M. 1990: Heirs apparent: Succession strategies for the future. *Personnel Management*, January.

Greller, M.M. 1978: The nature of subordinate participation in the ap- praisal interview. *Academy of Management Journal*, 12.

Greller, M.M. 1980: Evaluation of feedback sources as a function of role and organisational level. *Journal of Applied Psychology*, 65 (1).

Long, P. 1986: *Performance Appraisal Revisited*. London: IPM.

Mayo, A. 1991: *Managing Careers: Strategies for Organisations*. London: IPM.

Mohrman, A.M., Resnick-West, S.M. and Lawler, E.E. 1989: *Designing Performance Appraisal Systems*. San Francisco: Jossey-Bass.

Prince, J.B. and Lawler, E.E. 1986: Does salary discussion hurt the developmental performance appraisal? *Organisational Behaviour and Human Decision Processes*, 37.

Schein, E.H. 1978: *Career Dynamics: Matching Individual and Organizational Needs*. Reading, Mass.: Addison Wesley.

Wexley, K.N. and Klimoski, R. 1984 Performance appraisal: An update. In K.M. Rowland and G.R. Ferris *Research in Personnel and Human Resource Management*, Vol, 2, Greenwich, Conn.: JAI Press.

6

Implementation Issues

The importance of consultation and of involving as many managers and employees as possible during the design phase as a means of generating widely based interest and commitment was emphasized in the previous chapter. Equally, in the implementation phase, the process of consultation with as many individuals and groups should be continued, to ensure that all aspects of the performance appraisal system are fully communicated, and that practical 'nuts and bolts' issues are properly addressed.

Briefing

An essential condition for successful implementation is that all employees who will be involved, whether as appraisers or appraisees, should be fully briefed on the system. Ideally briefing should:

- Take place in face-to-face situations, in small groups, so that individuals will not feel inhibited to ask questions.
- Be reinforced through the written word, in the form of an explanatory booklet. Different versions of the booklet may be required for appraisers and appraisees.
- Provide a mechanism whereby individuals know whom to approach to answer questions which occur to them afterwards, or which they would prefer to have dealt with in private. This third aspect of briefing can often be developed into a kind of 'surgery service' to which either an appraiser or appraisee may have access. Such a service, provided by a human resource specialist or an external consultant, assists individuals by providing an interpretation of the organization's performance appraisal scheme, in terms of, for example, some difficult appraisal issue they are facing.

In terms of content, briefing should cover:

- The aims and objectives of the performance appraisal system.
- Benefits to key parties – appraisees, appraisers and the organization.
- Full details of the appraisal cycle, its various elements, including methods and documentation.
- Precisely what is expected of each party, at every stage in the performance appraisal cycle.
- The appraisal interview; its central importance.
- Appraisal outcomes: how the appraisal cycle is completed, what happens to appraisal data.

While briefing should take place for all employees involved at the launch of a new performance appraisal system, it is also appropriate to provide face-to-face briefings as part of induction training for recently recruited employees and for recently promoted employees who have now reached a level where they will be included in the system of performance appraisal.

Training

A number of studies have shown clearly that training has a major impact on the effectiveness of appraisal interviews. One of the recent trends has been to provide training for appraisees, so often the neglected party, as well as appraisers.

Dealing first with appraisers, the group to whom training is most likely to be given, clearly it is important to specify the range of areas where training is required. Typically, when an organization is introducing a new appraisal scheme, or modifying an old scheme, training for appraisers focuses on:

- Organization policy towards appraisal.
- The system and documents.
- Appraisal skills.

Some writers have advocated separating skills training, especially training in appraisal interviewing skills, from briefing on the system, to ensure there is sufficient emphasis on the appraisal process, so that skills acquisition is not distracted by discussion about systems and procedures.

While initially this separation can be justified, skills training can be enhanced, if at some point towards the end of the programme some attempt at integration is made.

If, for example, as part of the process of acquiring appraisal skills, the participants are required to take part in role-playing interviews, it can be useful to structure the role-playing into three phases:

1st stage: Simple role-playing, focusing on skills.
2nd stage: The role-playing now incorporates an element of appraisal documentation (e.g. the use of self-assessment documents).
3rd stage: The role-playing includes the completion of the organization's appraisal documents.

This gradual integration of skills development with new appraisal documents gives participants a better understanding of what is, or will be required of them as appraisers, and there is some evidence that this approach assists the transfer of learning from the training programmes back to the work situation.

Neglected issues in training

We will now look at issues that are often neglected in appraisal training.

Training appraisees It is pleasing to detect a recent trend of more organizations providing some form of training for appraisees.

The briefing of appraisees should help to alleviate anxieties, and indeed develop positive attitudes, in making appraisees aware of the benefits of performance appraisal. Fletcher (1984) has for long advocated the importance of giving appraisees training in self-assessment on the grounds that all through our educational backgrounds self-assessment is something that is infrequently encouraged. In addition, interview training for appraisees can be beneficial in preparing them to participate effectively in appraisal interviews. Role-playing is a useful technique in helping individuals to gain appraisal interviewing skills, and to understand issues from both appraiser and appraisee perspectives.

Training reviewers Another neglected area in training concerns the training of senior managers who are in a reviewing role – given that many appraisal systems require the 'grandfather' figure to play an important role, often in ensuring fairness and consistency in the appraisals of staff.

Timing of training An additional, often neglected issue concerns the timing of training. Typically, organizations quite rightly devote all training efforts when a new appraisal system is being launched. Some groups – appraisees especially but also appraisers and reviewers – would benefit from training after gaining appraisal experience. The issue of refresher training that can greatly assist in maintaining the momentum of training is often neglected. One major multinational organization has adopted the policy of training its managers in appraisal skills every two years. The importance of this policy was reinforced in studies of two large American multinationals where two-thirds of the managers surveyed indicated they felt they required some kind of refresher training in appraisal skills every two to three years.

Training in goal-setting   Many managers would certainly agree with Diane Bailey (1990) when she describes goal-setting as a crucial area to be covered in training programmes. For any organization making use of a results-oriented, objective-setting approach, the inclusion of a training element in goal-setting is recommended to ensure that appraisers fully understand the principle of goal-setting. Equipped with this knowledge and, hopefully, greater confidence, they should find it easier to develop appraisal interviews into a joint process, with the appraisee participating in the goal-setting.

Who should provide the training?

Organizations usually must make a choice between asking some of its own members – usually personnel and training staff, if it has a specialist human resource function – or inviting external parties, from professional management consulting companies or business schools. The decision will often depend on the extent to which expertise in the field of performance appraisal exists within the organization. Either internal or external providers can give satisfactory training.

Often, the most effective training is provided by using a mix of internal and external resources. The internal trainer has the advantage of knowing the organization, its culture, its staff, and its particular requirements; the external consultant can provide a breadth of vision and experience, and help to show to what extent the training challenges facing those who are attempting to gain new appraisal skills are similar to or different from those encountered in other organizations. The external consultant may be better placed to engage in dialogue with directors and very senior managers as a high-status third party. The downside risks are that some external consultants may tend to offer standard training packages. It is always important to establish to what extent an external consultant is willing to adapt training programmes, and develop new training approaches to meet the needs of the organization. Where good teamwork exists between external consultants and internal staff in providing training, the training programmes are most likely to be perceived as meeting the needs of appraisers and appraisees. In some organizations the role of the external consultant is to advise and help in the design phase, as well as in aspects of appraisal implementation, including training.

Pilot Studies

When a major new system of performance appraisal is introduced, especially if it involves major changes, some form of pilot exercise is usually advisable. This could involve introducing the scheme for the first appraisal cycle to one department or division to assess how well it is operating, and to rectify any teething problems before extending it more widely.

Cascade Approach

A closely related strategy adopted by many organizations occurs when they introduce a new appraisal scheme initially to senior management, then extend it at different time intervals to middle management, then to junior management, clerical staff and so on. This approach has the advantage of assessing how well it is working at higher levels in the organization; it also provides data to assist in assessing the desirability of extending the coverage of the system and the need for modifications when the system is applied to different categories of employees.

References

Bailey, D. 1990: Performance assessment, *The Training Officer*, March.
Fletcher, C.A. 1984: What's new in performance appraisal. *Personnel Management*, February.

7

Encouraging Employee Involvement

One of the major trends in designing and implementing systems of performance appraisal in recent years has been an increased emphasis on the importance of involving the appraisee in the operation of the system, particularly in terms of having the opportunity to make an input into his or her own appraisal. Increasingly in organizations the importance of securing the co-operation and commitment of the individual employee to the performance appraisal process is being recognized. Without positive co-operation and commitment on the part of the employee, any system of performance appraisal is in danger of failing if employees are distrustful of its purposes, fail to appreciate how it can benefit them and the organization, and behave in a negative and defensive fashion at appraisal interviews.

Employee Ownership of Appraisal

Lawrie (1989) argues that a strong case can be made for the inclusion of self-appraisal in systems of performance appraisal because it is the most powerful source of data on any employee's performance. Studies (e.g. Wexley, Singh and Yukl, 1973), show that the more the employee participates in the appraisal process the more satisfied he or she is likely to be with the appraisal interview and the appraiser, and the more likely it is that performance improvements will result. Fletcher and Williams (1985), while recognizing that research indicates that participation by the employee is positively correlated with favourable outcomes from the appraisal interview, sound a note of caution in asking what exactly participation means, and in suggesting that some forms of participation may be very superficial. Their view is that there is little point in employees airing their views at appraisal interviews unless there is a genuine willingness on the part of appraisers to listen to employees, and to be receptive to their ideas. Reinforcing this idea, Greller (1978) has suggested that only when the employee experiences feelings of ownership of the appraisal process does participation become effective in producing joint agreement on actions to solve problems and develop performance. To generate feelings of employee ownership of the appraisal process, effective employee involvement and participation can be generated in a number of ways, as outlined here.

At the design and initial implementation phase of the performance appraisal system

At this stage the employee should be involved in two ways:

In consultation sessions on the design of the system. The consultation process may be direct with groups of employees, or indirect, with representatives of employees. Direct consultation is a more powerful mechanism for generating employee interest in performance appraisal, and encouraging employees to suggest ideas for the design of the system.

In briefing sessions. These should cover the objectives of the performance appraisal system, the benefits to the key parties (including employees being appraised), and the role the various parties, including employees, are expected to play in the operation of the system.

Many writers (e.g. Yager, 1981) have stressed the importance of clarifying appraisal objectives. In addition, imparting an understanding of the benefits to all parties (Evenden and Anderson, 1992) is fundamental to securing their wholehearted support and cooperation. Talking employees through the various steps in the performance appraisal cycle and making clear the role they are expected to play at each stage removes uncertainties, reduces anxieties and increases understanding of the performance appraisal system.

At the pre-appraisal stage

Employee involvement at this stage can be encouraged by *completion of an interview preparation form* or by *completion of a self-assessment form.* Long (1986) rightly draws attention to the fact that these are not the same; many interview preparation forms, however, encourage self-assessment. Whatever the emphasis placed on self-assessment in the pre-interview document, it is likely to serve the useful purpose of encouraging employees to think about performance issues upon which they may not previously have reflected, and to make explicit their thoughts on a range of issues relating to their own performance. This stage should help to ensure that employees enter the appraisal interview in a state of readiness to participate and discuss constructively issues about their performance.

During the appraisal interview

If at least some, though it would be preferable if all, of the following conditions characterize the appraisal interview, it is highly probable that a very participative interview will take place, with the person being appraised making an active and effective contribution:

- An emphasis on problem identification and problem analysis, with the employee actively involved.
- The involvement of the employee in generating and evaluating courses of action, relating to solving problems, personal development, performance improvement and the setting of goals.
- A supportive and helpful interviewer, with good interpersonal skills in encouraging employee involvement, and in giving adequate freedom to the employee to express thoughts, feelings and ideas.
- A high percentage of interview time occupied by the employee doing the talking.
- A summary made by the employee outlining what actions he or she is prepared to make to improve performance and undertake personal development, also indicating future goals to which commitment is being given, with the agreement of the appraiser.
- Both parties maintaining good rapport throughout, no matter how candid the discussion or how difficult the issues.

While the style of the interviewer is clearly important in terms of how much employee involvement takes place in the appraisal interview, both the prevailing organizational culture in general, and the micro-culture of the unit of the organization in which appraiser and appraisee are located are likely to have a major impact on the extent to which trusting relationships can be established in the appraisal interview. Only if good trust levels exist will appraisees feel sufficiently free from anxiety and threats to participate willingly, to undertake honestly self-analysis and self-assessment, and to be proactive in problem-solving and in setting new goals and agreeing actions to develop performance.

After the appraisal interview

Participation will continue after the appraisal interview if the appraisee:

- is proactive in ensuring that actions agreed at the appraisal interview to improve performance are implemented, for example changes in working practices, improvements in managing time, new initiatives in dealing effectively with people and in acquiring new skills
- seeks meetings with the appraiser to gain feedback, advice and views on progress towards the achievement of goals
- suggests, when appropriate in the light of changing conditions, the need for a revision of previously agreed goals.

While these actions on the part of the appraisee indicate a high level of employee involvement and proactivity in the post-appraisal phase, the achievement of both improvements in the employee's performance and the development in the employee's abilities and skills will depend also on the extent to which the appraiser has developed effective coaching and counselling skills, the subject of chapter 11.

Problem Areas of Performance Appraisal

There are a number of problem areas of performance appraisal identified in the literature, e.g.:

- Identifying criteria for evaluating performance.
- Collecting accurate and comprehensive information about employee performance.
- Resolving conflict between appraiser and appraisee.
- Defensive behaviour exhibited by the appraisee can be overcome or minimized through the incorporation of a high degree of employee involvement and a self-review mechanism in the performance appraisal system, provided:

  - the major issues underlying employee involvement are faced up to, and resolved
  - certain basic conditions are established
  - there is a clear awareness of the assumptions on which the case for employee involvement and self-review is based.

Employees' Self-appraisal

Survey evidence (Long, 1986) suggests that during the 1980s many organizations have attempted to increase employee involvement in their performance appraisal systems through the introduction of interview preparation forms which the employee is invited or required to complete prior to the appraisal interview. Typically the employee is asked to provide data on the description of his or her job, recent changes in duties or priorities, his or her perception of job objectives and key tasks, and to comment on improvements in the current work situation, training and development needs, and his or her aspirations for the future.

The objective is usually to encourage the employee to undertake preparations for the appraisal interview, and to think carefully about issues influencing performance. Gill (1977) shows that 55 per cent of a large-scale survey of 30 per cent of UK-based organizations use interview preparation forms.

Her survey evidence indicated that around 28 per cent of these organizations attempt to build an element of self-assessment into these pre-appraisal forms. This development has a major impact on the appraisal system, and, in a sense, reverses the procedure. Instead of the manager, conventionally, making the evaluation and then imparting the contents to the employee, the employee initiates the procedure by providing evaluative comment on, for example, how well he or she has achieved tasks and objectives during the period under review; the problems that arose; and changes and improvements for the future.

This type of procedure, initiated by the employee, has important implications for the manager, who is now in a position to respond to the employee's self-assessment. In responding, if the manager wishes to modify the employee's self-evaluation, these comments are in addition to and not a replacement of what the employee has said. An examination of the literature (for example, Barnett and Anderson, 1985; Bassett and Meyer, 1968; McHenry, Howard and McHatton, 1984) suggests that where an element of self-appraisal is incorporated, the appraisal interview is likely to generate less inhibited and more positive discussion and provide a better climate for identifying problems, considering solutions and helping the individual to realize personal potential and develop career prospects.

As Margerison (1976) points out, the basic idea is not new. As long ago as 1960, McGregor was advocating that employees should undertake self-appraisal to assess how far they had accomplished targets established by mutual agreement with their managers. Of more recent origin, however, are some practical mechanisms devised by organizations to implement this philosophy towards appraisal. Many schemes now in operation have established a two-stage appraisal procedure. The first stage invites the employee to commit self-assessment to paper, and written answers are sought in response to the following questions:

Give a brief description of your job during the year of assessment.

Summarize the objectives set for you during the year of assessment.

State career objectives and how you see these objectives being fulfilled.

Give a brief summary of your performance during the year of assessment, together with achievements and difficulties encountered. Include also performance of any tasks which may fall outside your job description.

Indicate how any difficulties might have been remedied and also suggest how you might improve your performance.

The second stage, the manager's written evaluation of the employee, requires the manager to provide ratings of things such as quality of work, motivation, professional skill/competence, ability to communicate, and management of staff. In addition, the manager is asked to comment on the employee's effectiveness in his or her present job, performance in relation to agreed objectives, strengths and weaknesses, career prospects and training requirements.

Two examples of self-assessment forms used by companies are shown in appendix 7.1 and appendix 7.2.

The nature of self-appraisal

A number of important issues are likely to have a considerable bearing on the precise nature of systems involving self-appraisal and their successful implementation.

Sequence of stages in the appraisal procedure Should the self-assessment prepared by the employer be submitted to the manager in advance, so that it becomes one of the information inputs used by the manager in deliberating over the completion of the appraisal of the employee? Alternatively, should each party complete their reports independently, with the implication that the main part of the agenda for the appraisal interview becomes the examination and discussion of points of difference in their respective viewpoints, with a view to reconciling as many of these differences as possible?

Of these alternatives, the first, despite the lack of survey evidence, appears to have become the more widely adopted practice. It could be argued, however, that it is more open to the distortions of bias, in that the appraiser may be over-influenced (in either a positive or negative way) by the employee's self-assessment submitted in advance. The second alternative is likely to make greater demands on the manager's interviewing skills, since there will be a higher degree of unpredictability about the discussion in the appraisal interview, if the manager has no prior knowledge of the employee's self-evaluation. Submitting completed self-assessment documents in advance to appraisers seems, on balance, to be the preferred option.

The permanence of the documentation Gill (1977) has reported resistance on the part of some employees towards interview preparation forms and self-appraisal methods in situations where the self-appraisal documents are retained with other parts of the appraisal documentation in their personal files. Employees may feel they cannot be fully honest in committing the appraisal of their own performance to writing, out of fear that the information may be used to their detriment in future decisions on, for example, promotions, transfers, training or salary decisions.

On the other hand, if the self-appraisal document does not have the same status as other appraisal documents, and is not to be retained, there is the danger that it will not be taken seriously by either appraiser or appraisee.

Many organizations have overcome this issue by letting employees choose whether or not they wish their self-assessment documents to be retained and attached to the documentation completed by their appraisers.

The timing of the introduction of self-appraisal Any change in appraisal procedures, e.g. the introduction of self-assessment, must be planned to reduce threat to those involved. It is clearly desirable that any such change should take place at a time when the organization is expanding rather than contracting, and fears of insecurity and job loss are at a minimum. It may be possible, however, to introduce changes successfully into appraisal systems during adverse economic conditions, provided certain key conditions are established.

Conditions for the effective use of self-assessment

A wide range of factors, relating both to the appraisal system, and to the environment (e.g. the business and managerial climates, the organization structure and technology) will have an impact on the introduction of self-appraisal mechanisms into the appraisal system. Some of the more important conditions are identified below.

Nature and clarity of appraisal objectives It is generally recognized that appraisal schemes can be designed to serve a range of different objectives. The appropriateness of self-appraisal is likely to depend on the particular objectives set, and the priorities established among these objectives. Where a primary aim, as in the case of many US and some British schemes is to assist in the distribution of organization rewards, self-appraisal may become a difficult or even counter-productive mechanism to operate, since individuals, it could be argued, will attempt to develop tactics to secure the best possible ratings to maximize their rewards, rather than in producing an open, honest and frank self-evaluation of their own performance.

Self-appraisal appears to be most readily adopted where primary emphasis is placed on the objective of encouraging the development of employees (Fletcher and Williams, 1985).

Emphasis on the future The more strongly an appraisal scheme is concerned with the future, the more powerful are the arguments for using self-appraisal. If employees feel the major purpose of appraisal is on the past, they may be inclined to attempt to describe their own performance in unduly favourable terms. On the other hand, a more candid, frank self-assessment will emerge if it is known that the main objective is to analyse past performance and learn from both successes and failures as a basis for setting realistic objectives for the future.

Employee awareness of responsibility for self-development Temporal (1981) suggests that the literature on employee development has often given the impression that learning and development are highly structured and dependent on the outcomes of a range of planned learning experiences such as formal training courses, instead of being a continuous process. Temporal postulates that a large part of learning and development takes place under conditions that are not planned or deliberate. This view appears to harmonize with Drucker's (1974) comment that the only path to effective development is through self-development, on the grounds that motivation, leading to the realization of an individual's abilities and strengths, must come from within. Hodson (1981) indicates a wide range of factors which are likely to influence the pattern of self-development. An issue of central importance is the correct internal perception of the challenge facing the individual. As Hodson points out, the prefix 'self' has two distinct meanings. First, it indicates that it is the self, or the person, who is being developed, as distinct from the organization or business. Secondly, it indicates that the impetus to development is self-initiated.

If self-assessment mechanisms are to contribute to the important appraisal objective of encouraging the development of the individual, it is a vital precondition that, in the light of the findings in the literature, employees have a correct understanding of the factors that lead to successful development. The greater the willingness of employees to accept responsibility for their own development, based on the notions of self-motivation and the belief that development is a continuous process, the greater the likelihood that they will respond positively and honestly to self-assessment. The discussion in the appraisal interview will provide an opportunity for employees to test their internal perception of the development challenges facing them against the views of their managers.

Provision of training in appraisal methodology and appraisal interviewing
Despite widespread agreement in the literature on the need to train managers in appraisal techniques and appraisal interviewing skills, Gill (1977) reports that a disappointingly low number of organizations actually do provide such training. She indicates that although 56 per cent of the responding organizations stated they provided appraisal training for their managers, 67 per cent agreed with the statement elsewhere in the survey questionnaire that 'appraisal interviews are of little value unless accompanied by appropriate training'. This discrepancy between practice and belief seems to characterize the ambivalent attitude of many organizations towards performance appraisal, and the provision of training in appraisal skills.

Self-appraisal makes new demands on managers in their role as the conductor of the appraisal interview, and a manager without adequate training is likely to find the interview a difficult situation to handle. As already noted, when a self-assessment mechanism is incorporated into the appraisal scheme managers find themselves in a situation where they can respond to, and add to, the views and comment of employees without having to initiate the evaluative comment. Margerison (1976) suggests that in this situation the manager should adopt a joint problem-solving approach, focusing on the identification and exploration of the key problems facing the employee, and encouraging the employee to think through the issues involved.

This clearly demands considerable interpersonal skills on the part of the manager, as well as a thorough understanding of the objectives and mechanisms of the appraisal system.

Where the appraisal scheme is designed to include an element of self-appraisal, the manager's interviewing skills, to ensure that effective use is made of the evaluative comment provided by both parties, should be directed towards:

- Allowing freedom for the employee to do at least half of the talking.
- Being sensitive to feelings (with the interviewer attempting to interpret the feelings that lie behind the employee's words).
- Giving and receiving feedback, with the interviewer as well as the appraisee attempting to profit from the feedback which the interpersonal communication of the appraisal interview provides.

Self-appraisal puts extra demands on appraisees. In order to put forward useful factual and evaluative comment about their performance during the period under review, they require a clear understanding of the aims, mechanisms and processes of the appraisal system. Without training, the likelihood of appraisees demonstrating commitment to the scheme will probably be reduced.

Trust and confidence in manager–employee relationships Unless a high level of mutual trust and confidence characterizes manager–employee relationships, it is unlikely that individuals will be able, without feelings of threat, to participate in a positive way in an appraisal scheme that utilizes self-appraisal. The research findings of Nemeroff and Wexley (1979) indicate that the greater the extent that the manager adopts the role of helper and shows respect for the employee as a person, the higher the degree of employee satisfaction with the appraisal process.

Conclusions

Self-appraisal is still viewed with suspicion by some practitioners. There is a growing body of theoretical and empirical evidence to suggest that self-appraisal:

Overcomes many of the traditional problems of performance appraisal It improves the flow of relevant, accurate information to appraisers; it assists in resolving uncertainties about criteria for job success; it is likely to reduce defensive behaviour and have a positive effect on employee motivation by involving employees in an active way in the appraisal process.

Encourages better preparation for appraisal interviews, especially by making appraisees think carefully about their roles, relationships, problems and performance.

Helps develop more positive attitudes towards performance appraisal in many, though admittedly not all, situations on the part of both appraiser and appraisee, through the active involvement of both parties.

Generates a proactive approach to development whereby employees recognize the need for not only the self-evaluation of current performance but also accept a measure of responsibility for identifying their own training needs and planning and organizing their own development requirements.

A number of conditions must be achieved for effective self-appraisal to take place with a system of performance appraisal. The most important of these are the establishment of good levels of trust and open communications between appraisers and appraisees.

References

Barnett, J.G. and Anderson, G.C. 1985: *Nursing Staff Development Programme: An Enquiry into the Effectiveness of the Appraisal Interview.* Edinburgh: Scottish Health Service Management Development Group.

Bassett, G.A. and Meyer, H.H. 1968: Performance Appraisal Based on Self-Review. *Personnel Psychology*, 21.

Drucker, P. 1974: *Management: Tasks, Responsibilities, Practices.* London: Heinemann.

Evenden, R. and Anderson, G.C. 1992: *Management Skills: Making the Most of People.* London: Addison Wesley.

Fletcher, C.A. and Williams, R. 1985: *Performance Appraisal and Career Development.* London: Hutchinson.

Gill, D. 1977: *Appraising Performance.* London: IPM.

Greller, M.M. 1978: The nature of subordinate participation in the appraisal interview. *Academy of Management Journal,* 21 (4).

Hodson, P. 1981: Stimulating self-development. In T. Boydell and M. Pedlar (eds), *Management Self-Development: Concepts and Practices.* London: Gower.

Lawrie, J.W. 1989: Your performance: appraise it yourself! *Personnel,* January.

Long, P. 1986: *Performance Appraisal Revisited.* London: IPM.

McGregor, D. 1960: *The Human Side of Enterprise.* Now York: McGraw-Hill.

McHenry, R., Howard, J. and McHatton, M. 1984: Employee-driven personnel appraisal. Paper delivered at the Institute of Personnel Management National Conference, Harrogate.

Margerison, C. 1976: A constructive approach to appraisal. *Personnel Management,* 8 (7), July.

Nemeroff, W.F. and Wexley, K.N. 1979: An exploration of the relationship between performance feedback interview characteristics and interview outcomes as perceived by managers and subordinates. *Journal of Occupational Psychology,* 52.

Temporal, P. 1981: Creating the climate for self-development. In T. Boydell and M. Pedlar (eds), *Management Self-Development: Concepts and Practices.* London: Gower.

Wexley, K.N., Singh, J.B. and Yukl, G.A. 1973: Subordinate personality as a moderator of the effects of participation in three types of appraisal interviews. *Journal of Applied Psychology,* 58 (1).

Yager, E. 1981: A critique of performance appraisal systems. *Personnel Journal,* February.

Appendix 7.1 Example A of a self-assessment form

Name: .... **Date:** ....

Job Title: .... **Department:** ....

Describe, in the space below the main purpose of your job.

Which aspects of your job do you feel you have done well, during the review period?

Describe any difficulties you may have had, and how you overcame them.

Describe any external factors which may have helped, or hindered your job performance.

Which areas of your job performance do you feel could be improved by you, or with the help of your manager? Please state actions which you feel should be taken, and by whom.

What work objectives would you consider to be important to achieve, over the next year?

Does your job fully utilize your abilities? If not, how could your skills be used more fully?

List any additional qualifications you have achieved during the review period, and any courses you have attended.

In what way would you like your career to develop over the next year?

What personal development would you hope to achieve:

(a) during the next year?

(b) in the longer term?

Signature: .... Date: ....

Appendix 7.2   Example B of a self-assessment form

PERFORMANCE APPRAISAL & DEVELOPMENT PROGRAMME

INTERVIEW PREPARATION FORM

Name of Appraisee: _____   Designation: _____

Division/Location: _____   Duration In
                                       The Job: _____

Your manager has asked you to participate in a performance appraisal and development discussion. The purpose of the discussion is to constructively examine your performance and identify areas in which further development should take place.

The subject of the discussion is YOU – your performance, your development needs and your aspirations. It is very important that your views are communicated to your Manager in advance of the discussion. This form will enable both of you to prepare for the discussion and hence ensure that it is mutually constructive and useful.

Please be totally honest and frank in answering the questions. After completion, hand it over to your manager at least three days before the discussion. This will give him or her time to also prepare for the discussion.

Please do not discuss your answers with your colleagues. This is a confidential document and should be treated as such.

Part 1. Your Job

1. What is the aim of your job?

2. What are the main tasks to be carried out in your job?

3. Describe the most frequently occurring types of problems you have to tackle in your job. List them in order of frequency.

4. What are the most important things you have achieved in your job in the last twelve months?

5. What do you hope to achieve in your job in the next twelve months?

Part 2. Improving Your Performance

1. Are there obstacles hindering you from accomplishing what you would wish? List them.

2. Do you need more knowledge of particular topics? List them.

3. Are there skills which you should try to acquire or improve by training?

4. What skills do you possess now which are not being used to the fullest in your job?

5. Identify ways/areas in which your effectiveness could be enhanced and you become more satisfied in your job.

Part 3. Future

1. In what ways would you like to see your own career develop within the next 3 years? What are your personal objectives? Indicate, for example, if you would prefer to be in a completely different area.

2. Any other comments?

Appraisee's Signature: Date:

8

Operating the Performance Appraisal System: The Importance of the Appraisal Interview

Most appraisal schemes include provision for the holding of appraisal interviews which provide an opportunity for managers to discuss with employees their performance and to develop plans for the future. The appraisal interview is seen increasingly by organizations as the key feature that will determine the success or failure of the performance appraisal system.

This is illustrated in the chapter of case studies (chapter 13) when the appraisal interview is seen as the central element in the systems described. As noted in earlier chapters, in most systems the immediate line manager has the responsibility for undertaking appraisal interviews; the role of personnel and training specialists is generally to support line managers in carrying out this function through briefing, advice and the provision of training programmes.

The appraisal interview is one of the most difficult forms of interview which a manager is asked to undertake because:

- The interview can be extremely unpredictable, especially over matters relating to areas of deficient performance and the weaknesses of the individual.
- The manager must display a wide range of interpersonal skills in conducting effective appraisal interviews.
- Appraisal interviewing skills cannot be readily learned from watching other managers in action. Because of the confidential nature of the appraisal interview, it is unlikely that a manager will witness anyone else in the role of the interviewer except his or her own manager.

Most organizations, from both public and private sectors, adopt the view that the appraisal interview, because of the inevitably sensitive and personal nature of discussions about individual performance should be conducted 'one-to-one'.

Line managers may perceive performance appraisal as a task that should be carried out by personnel managers or by a personnel specialist (Parkinson, 1977). The widely held current view is that personnel managers are unlikely to be the best people to carry out appraisal interviews, not because they lack the necessary skills, but because they have no direct formal and continuous relationship with the employees subject to appraisal. Appraisal interviewing, therefore, is most appropriately carried out by line managers, since performance appraisal is an integral feature of management.

Length of the Appraisal Interview

The effectiveness of interviews cannot obviously be judged according to the amount of time devoted to them, but the data in table 8.1 derived from the UK IPM 1977 and 1986 surveys highlights wide variations in practice. Clearly this data must be interpreted with caution, since it was impossible for respondents to know exact times for their organizations, and the length of interview is likely to vary both within the organization and for the same interviewer. In addition, some of the organizations involved in the surveys did not feel able to answer the question.

If appraisal is carried out with conviction and commitment, it is likely to make considerable demands on managerial time, and the evidence suggests that in some organizations substantial amounts of time are devoted to appraisal interviews. On the other hand, the small amount of time allocated to appraisal interviews in admittedly a minority of organizations, suggests that in those organizations there is less than total commitment to performance appraisal, and that the appraisal process has probably become superficial and ritualistic. In the later survey, one to two hours emerges as the most likely length of a manager's appraisal interview.

Objectives of the Appraisal Interview

The appraisal interview can serve a number of objectives. These should relate to the overall objectives which the organization expects

Table 8.1 Time devoted to the appraisal interview for managerial staff

Time	Percentage of organizations	
	1977	*1986*
Up to ½ hour	19	3
½–1 hour	34	27
1–2 hours	26	53
Over 2 hours	7	15
Not known	14	3

Sources: Gill (1977) and Long (1986)

its performance appraisal scheme as a whole to achieve and are likely to include:

Letting the employee know where he or she stands. This is most readily achieved in an open appraisal system which encourages appraisers to exchange feedback with appraisees in an honest and candid way.

Providing an opportunity for a discussion about the employee's job performance over the period under review. This emphasizes the need for a two-way exchange of information, with appraisers explaining and amplifying the contents of the appraisal report, and employees putting forward their point of view.

Agreeing action to improve the performance of the employee. The discussion of performance should lead to the agreement of a number of actions, not only by the appraisee but also by the appraiser to improve current performance. It can also lead to the consideration of career prospects in the organization, the employee's ambitions, and training and development required to realize the employee's potential, both in the present job and also as preparation for future positions.

How Appropriate are Appraisal Interviews?

Anstey and Fletcher (1976) suggest that the term 'the appraisal interview' is to some extent misleading. The emphasis should be on a problem-solving approach to overcoming difficulties, not simply on providing the employee with evaluative comments on past performance, important though this is. Indeed, many organizations have now renamed appraisal interviews as 'performance reviews' or 'development sessions', or have given them some other title which does not include the word 'appraisal'.

Some authors have argued that appraisal interviews serve no useful purpose. Scepticism about the values of the appraisal interview is often extended to the total concept of performance appraisal. Pym (1973), for example, has questioned whether appraisal interviews are necessary under any circumstances, arguing that 'appraisal represents an organizational attempt to ride rough-shod over what is frequently a tenuous and precarious relationship'. He emphasizes the potential harm to working relationships, and damaging effects of the formalization of appraisal. He considers appraisal and appraisal interviews as 'rituals of employment' which provide no organizational or individual benefit. While what Pym has to say may be true of bad performance appraisal systems, it is questionable whether this is universally true. His comments are of value in pointing to the need for both careful preparation prior to appraisal interviews and follow-up action, without which the interviews become an irrelevant activity.

Links between Formal and Informal Appraisal

A common line of argument often put forward by practitioners who are sceptical about performance appraisal is to stress that appraisal interviewing on an informal basis is an integral part of day-to-day management and supervision. Good supervisors and managers will therefore regularly monitor the performance of staff, indicating defects that call for correction, and providing encouragement to build on strengths. Formal appraisal interviews, according to this line of reasoning, are consequently superfluous and time-consuming.

This view runs counter to the research findings of Fletcher (1978), who has focused attention on the normal working relationship between managers and subordinates, and the influence of this on performance appraisal. His broad conclusion is that the more managers talk over employees' work with them, the more likely it is that managers will conduct appraisal interviews that are perceived as having positive effects on job performance and job satisfaction.

This contradicts the view that if we have good communications the rest of the time, we do not require appraisal interviews. Fletcher's findings help to demonstrate the importance of regular, informal appraisal and counselling sessions involving manager and employee, not as a replacement for, but in addition to formal appraisal interviews, and this theme is developed in chapter 11.

Preparation

The importance of planning for appraisal interviews has received considerable attention in the literature. Buzzota and Lefton (1979) argue that any appraisal interview held without planning will at best waste time and money. At worst it may lead to a decrease in productivity. Poorly planned appraisal interviews are likely to have damaging effects on employee morale and motivation.

There should be a planning stage in which both appraiser and appraisee identify the appraisee's job goals. Both parties should agree the goals which will be discussed during the appraisal interview, to ensure that both enter the interview prepared to talk on the same wavelength. This approach stresses that before the interview each party should attempt an evaluation of which goals have been attained and which have not.

The next stage involves analysing each goal using four criteria:

1. Was the goal too easy, too difficult or too vague?
2. What did the employee do that contributed to the goal being achieved or missed?
3. What did the manager contribute?
4. What external factors have altered, influencing the probability of achieving the goal?

The ensuing stages should consider several questions:

- In what way has achievement or non-achievement of the goal affected the employee, the organization and the manager?
- Has anything happened to change the employee's duties or business objectives from now on?
- What will the employee have to do to achieve maximum effectiveness in future?

This approach to planning – if carried out by both parties – should permit appraiser and appraisee to enter the appraisal interview with provisional answers to these three questions:

1. How effective is the employee's job performance?
2. What are the factors influencing this performance?
3. What changes should be made?

Styles of Interview

A wide variety of styles considered appropriate for conducting appraisal interviews have been discussed in the literature. Probably the best-known classification of appraisal interviewing styles has emerged from the work of the American industrial psychologist the late Norman Maier (1958). Maier put forward three main styles of appraisal interviewing:

The tell and sell approach   This style is likely to be adopted by interviewers who have an authoritarian approach to management. Interviewers concentrate on telling employees the evaluation that has been made of their performance, and then attempt to convince the employees of the fairness of the assessment, and the need for them to accept whatever follow-up action is recommended. The main deficiencies of this approach are the one-way nature of communications, the defensive response which this style is likely to evoke from employees, and the consequent difficulty of securing their commitment to the follow-up action which appraisers attempt to impose upon them.

The tell and listen approach   Interviewers still attempt to convey their evaluation to employees, but some attempt is made to develop two-way communication by encouraging employees to express their views, and respond to the evaluation made of their work performance. This may be an improvement on the 'tell and sell' method, but it still suffers the drawback that employees may feel forced into a defensive position, on hearing how the appraiser has evaluated their performance.

The problem-solving approach   Under this approach, the appraiser starts the interview by encouraging the employee to identify and discuss problem areas and then consider solutions. The employee therefore plays an active part in analysing problems and suggesting solutions, and the evaluation of performance emerges from the discussion at the appraisal interview, instead of being imposed by the appraiser upon the employee. This approach is essentially problem-centred rather than solution-centred. With the problem solving approach the emphasis is less on what went right or wrong with performance in the past, and more on ensuring that steps are taken to improve performance in the future.

Maier suggests that, as far as possible, managers should abandon the 'Tell and sell' and 'Tell and listen' styles and adopt the 'Problem-solving' approach.

The Interview Process

An examination of the literature suggests that attention has largely focused on the following interview process characteristics:

A substantial element of employee participation in the appraisal process Studies (e.g. Wexley, Singh and Yukl, 1973) show that the more the employee participates in the appraisal process, the more satisfied he or she is likely to be with the interview and the interviewer, and the more likely are performance improvements to take place resulting from the appraisal interview. The quality of the participation is important, in terms of the extent the employee feels able to express ideas and attitudes.

A positive and supportive approach by the interviewer In general, the greater the extent to which the style of the interviewer follows positive motivational principles, including showing an appreciation of the appraisee's point of view, helping in constructive fashion in resolving job problems and giving praise for achievements, the more likely the employee will respond favourably to the appraisal interview and act on the actions agreed. The importance of avoiding negative criticism was stressed in the classic study by Meyer, Kay and French (1965), while the need for a climate of trust, openness and constructiveness in the appraisal interview has been highlighted in more recent investigations (e.g. Lawler, Mohrman and Resnick-West, 1984).

Identifying and analysing problems affecting the employee's job performance Maier (1958), as previously noted, in an early study indicated that interviews characterized by joint problem solving, focusing on real job problems encountered by the employee, were more likely to lead to positive outcomes in terms of satisfaction with the interview and subsequent performance improvement. Margerison (1976) contends that a key factor in appraisal interviews is the extent to which they are problem-, rather solution-centred. The greater the effort and emphasis devoted to identifying and analysing the nature of problems, the more likely that changes in behaviour and performance will occur, compared with situations where appraisers impose solutions.

The setting of goals to be achieved by the employee The setting of specific goals which the employee will seek to attain has been shown to have a more powerful effect on subsequent performance than a general discussion about goals. An important factor concerns the process by which specific goals are set – the greater the extent that both parties participate in setting goals, the more likely that the employee will show commitment to their achievement. Greller (1978) states that the most important factor in conducting a successful appraisal interview is the creation of a sense of ownership by the appraisee. Brinkerhoff and Kanter (1980) suggest that this sense of ownership is generated through collaborative goal-setting.

The balance in the interview discussion between job performance and personality of the employee   Studies (e.g. Rothaus, Morton and Hanson, 1965), have shown that where there is greater emphasis on job performance rather than on the personality of the individual, more satisfaction with the interview is likely to be expressed by both parties, with greater motivation on the part of the employee to develop performance.

Relating Interview Process to Interview Outcomes: Case Study

A research study was carried out in the National Health Service to review the effectiveness of appraisal interviews among nursing staff (see Barnett and Anderson, 1985; Anderson and Barnett, 1986, 1987).

The central purpose of this study was to follow the research strategy of Burke, Weitzel and Weir (1978) in examining the influence of a number of interview process characteristics on a range of interview outcomes.

The six dependent variables or outcomes of the appraisal interviewing process largely replicate the measures used in previous studies, and cover a range of areas, including satisfaction with the appraisal process and impacts of the appraisal interview on the attitude, behaviour and performance of the employee.

Because of the important role of preparation for the appraisal interview identified in many previous studies (e.g. Buzzota and Lefton, 1979), and the recent trends towards the inclusion of elements of self-assessment discussed by Long (1986), an additional aim has been to examine the effects of pre-interview preparation and self-assessment documentation completed by the job holder on the various interview process and outcome measures. Other aims include the consideration of the relationship of length with the process and outcome measures, including actions agreed and later implemented, the lack of follow-up action having been so frequently a source of criticism about appraisal interviews (see, for example, Gill, 1977).

Method

Subjects The respondents were 317 nursing staff from one Scottish Health Board (Fife). Tables 8.2–8.6 display the demographic characteristics of the sample. There is considerable diversity, with a wide range evident on each demographic variable. Thus, the sample included respondents from many different nursing levels, from enrolled nurse to director of nursing services, and also from a wide range of nursing functions. Ages varied widely, with 11.5 per cent under twenty-six years and 37.2 per cent over forty-five years. A fairly stable employment pattern is evident with only 3.3 per cent of the sample indicating that they had less than six months' service in their present job, and 45.7 per cent with over five years in their present job.

Procedure The collection of data resulted from a twelve-page questionnaire completed by a stratified sample of nursing personnel drawn from different organizational levels in the Fife Health Board. One of the authors, then Nursing Adviser to the Scottish Health Service's Management Education and Training Division (subsequently renamed the Scottish Health Services Management Development Group), visited each unit of management and the College of Nursing and Midwifery, accompanied by the Area Nursing Officer (Staff Development). The background to, and proposed conduct of, the study was explained to the Directors of Nursing Service, the Director of Nurse Education and representatives of the qualified staff. Their assistance was sought for the distribution of questionnaires to 388 nurses selected from lists of staff submitted by each director. An individual letter explaining the study was enclosed with each questionnaire. Respondents were given approximately three weeks to reply, and were asked to return their questionnaires direct to the Management Education and Training Division in Edinburgh.

Of the 388 forms sent out, 317 were returned completed and 16 were sent back blank but with an explanatory note. This gave an exceptionally good response rate of 83 per cent. Items in the questionnaire were addressed to the most recent appraisal interview experienced by the respondents, in the role of both appraisee and,

Tables 8.2–8.6 Demographic characteristics of NHS case study sample

Table 8.2 Nursing function

Nursing function	%
Community	24.0
General	23.7
Geriatric	16.4
Psychiatry	14.1
Midwifery	10.5
Education	3.3
Mental handicap	6.3
Other	1.6

n = 317

Table 8.3 Present post

Present post	%
Director/assistant director of nursing services	2.0
Senior nurse	11.5
Charge nurse/ward sister	21.4
Health visitor	10.9
Staff nurse/staff midwife	20.1
District nurse (RGN)	10.5
Senior enrolled/enrolled nurse	18.8
Senior tutor/tutor	2.3
Clinical teacher	2.6

n = 317

Table 8.4 Age

Age	%
Under 26	11.5
26–35	22.7
36–45	28.3
Over 45	37.2

n = 317

Table 8.5 Length of time in present job

Length of time in present job	%
Under 6 months	3.3
6 months to 1 year	7.2
1 year to 3 years	22.0
3 years to 5 years	21.1
5 years or more	45.7

n = 317

Table 8.6 Length of time in present grade

Length of time in present grade	%
Under 6 months	2.3
6 months to 1 year	6.3
1 year to 3 years	20.1
3 years to 5 years	15.5
5 years or more	55.6

n = 317

where appropriate, appraiser. Thus, responses were based on recollection and perception. The Scottish Nursing Staff Development Programme requests that each member of staff be appraised on a yearly basis.

Measures

Interview process variables   Five measures of interview process characteristics similar to those described earlier in this chapter assessed on four-point Likert scales, were examined.

1. *Supportiveness of interviewer*: 'At your (most recent) appraisal interview how did you find your senior officer's attitude?'
2. *Balance between job performance and personality*: 'To what extent was the emphasis in the interview discussion placed on your job performance – or on your personality?'
3. *Influence*: 'Were you able to put forward and discuss your ideas and feelings at the interview?'
4. *Solving job problems*: 'Were real job problems sorted out at the interview?'
5. *Goal setting*: 'Was agreement reached on actions to achieve specific results?'

Interview outcome variables   Six outcomes of the appraisal interview were examined, again using four-point Likert scales:

1. *Relevance to patient care*: 'How relevant was the interview discussion to improving nursing service/patient care standards?'
2. *Motivation*: 'At the end of the interview did you feel encouraged or discouraged?'
3. *Perceived fairness*: 'How fair was your senior officer's assessment of your performance?'
4. *Performance improvement*: 'Has your performance improved following your last appraisal interview?'
5. *Perceived importance of the appraisal interview*: 'How much importance do you attach to the interview?'
6. *Impact on superior–subordinate relations*: 'Has the interview had any impact on relations between you and your senior officer?'

Findings

A number of highly positive findings from nursing staff emerged about performance appraisal. The three most significant were:

Table 8.7   Action to develop performance

Action intended	Number planning to take this action (n = 304)	Number that actually took this action
Attendance at formal course	142	89
Coaching	66	41
Visits	67	31
Temporary attachments	31	21
Use of reference materials	65	52
Self-development	110	75

- Satisfaction with the conduct of the appraisal interview.
- Perceived fairness and enhanced motivation.
- The setting up of a wide range of actions to develop staff performance.

One of the most encouraging findings of the survey was the generally positive set of employee responses towards the way appraisal interviews, in general, are handled. The majority of participants (54 per cent) reported that they found their senior officer's attitude at the appraisal interview highly supportive, and a further (25 per cent) found it slightly supportive. Most of those involved in the survey indicated that they enjoyed considerable freedom in putting forward and discussing their ideas and feelings at the appraisal interview. The majority of survey participants indicated that their senior officer's assessment of their performance was extremely fair. Further, the majority indicated positive links between the appraisal interview and motivation, stating that, on the whole they felt encouraged at the end of the interview.

A major positive finding is that a wide range of actions to develop performance were agreed by staff with their managers at the appraisal interview. Encouragingly, a substantial number of the activities planned were subsequently implemented, as shown in table 8.7.

Although attendance at formal courses elicited most mentions, an interesting feature is that in many cases alternative approaches to employee development were planned and implemented. In particular, self-development, coaching, temporary attachments, visits to other nursing units and the provision of reference materials all gained considerable mention. While inevitably some of the planned activities did not take place, more than half did, except in the case of visits to other nursing units, where the success rate was lower.

Several mixed and less positive findings also emerged. Respondents' views towards the appraisal interview's importance and its perceived relevance to improved job performance and better health care standards are much more problematical. In this area of the survey a mixed pattern of responses emerged. Only 47 per cent of respondents rated the appraisal interview as being of reasonable or substantial importance to them.

Views of the interview discussion's relevance to improving nursing service/patient care standards were extremely mixed – 47 per cent indicating either some or substantial relevance, but 40.8 per cent saw only slight or no relevance.

Service staff who have discussed these findings, consider that the individual staff member being the focus of attention may account for the lack of perception of the discussion's relevance to patient care.

Indeed this may be reflected in the response to the question on benefits of the programme – 'at last, time for me'. This could be a timely reminder to managers faced with failing standards or morale.

More disturbingly negative is the view of a sizeable group (50.4 per cent of respondents) who consider that their performance has improved only slightly or hardly at all because of the appraisal interview. And just under a fifth 'didn't know' whether their performance has altered because of the appraisal. This suggests a need for informal counselling as a key part of the staff development.

A disappointingly large number (33 per cent) estimated that their most recent appraisal interview took less than twenty-five minutes. It seems most unlikely that meaningful, in-depth discussions reviewing a whole year's work and planning for the year ahead could take place in such a short time. A further 32 per cent indicated between twenty-five and forty minutes as the length of their appraisal interviews.

This data compares unfavourably with the findings of IPM data covering a wide variety of organizations' appraisal practices shown in table 8.1. This showed that most appraisal interviews of managerial staff last for between one and two hours. To avoid a totally unfair comparison, it should be noted that under half of the NHS sample could be classified as holding managerial positions. The survey responses reveal a small group (5–7 per cent) aggrieved about most aspects of the appraisal interview. They felt they were unfairly assessed; they felt discouraged after the appraisal interview and saw few opportunities to express their views at the interview. It is disturbing to find so many people with such a negative approach to appraisal interviewing.

The most striking feature of the senior nursing staff appraisers are their generally positive views towards the appraisal interview, and commitment towards its success. A high degree of conscientiousness is indicated by the substantial amount of time devoted to preparation for appraisal.

The majority (52 per cent) of those in the sample who conduct appraisal interviews devote between a half and one hour to interview preparation, for each member of their staff. A substantial number (31 per cent) indicated they spent between one and two hours in preparation for each interview.

The great majority of appraisers perceived the interview as a two-way exchange of views in which the employee being interviewed plays a full and active part. Few (only 17 per cent) admitted to encountering difficulties in planning for, or conducting interviews. They also, generally, recognized the value of the review form as an aid to planning and conducting appraisal interviews.

But in view of the fact that 65 per cent of appraisees used the pre-interview, self-assessment form and overall found it an aid to discussion, increased benefits may have arisen had more time been devoted to the actual interview.

A desire to further develop their appraisal interviewing effectiveness can be seen in the fact that though many have undergone various forms of training, a large proportion recognize the need for further training:

Percentage receiving training before conducting interviews:

Objectives and operations – 62%
Completion of forms – 58%
Interviewing skills – 48%
Coaching skills – 16%

Percentage requesting further training:

Objectives and operations – 36%
Completion of forms – 23%
Interviewing skills – 43%
Coaching skills – 62%

That so many appraisers recognize the need for training in coaching skills shows they are increasingly aware of the importance of the connection between regular coaching which goes on at the place of work and the formal performance appraisal programme.

The central conclusion appears to be that although nurses mainly have positive views towards the appraisal interview processes, there is not universal and wholehearted commitment to the importance and relevance of the appraisal interview to improve job performance and organizational efficiency. Many nurses see appraisal as being principally concerned with the development of careers and preparation for promotion, rather than with the improvement of performance in the present job. It may be the case that this survey's main finding is that the mechanics of performance appraisal are working reasonably well, but more must be done to communicate the formal appraisal programme's objectives to all involved. The analysis highlights some apparent paradoxes: the substantial amount of preparation carried out by many appraisees and appraisers, and yet the apparent shortness of most appraisal interviews; the very mixed views on the individual and organizational importance of the appraisal interview despite the fact that a wide range of useful actions are planned, and in many cases, carried out; and few appraisers admitting to problems yet many expressing the need for further training.

A number of training implications have emerged from this. They include the need to communicate the objectives of the nursing staff development programme more effectively to everyone; organizing follow-up activities to ensure actions agreed in the appraisal interview take place; periodic training to reinforce the effects of earlier training to ensure that people are reminded of what is involved in achieving effectiveness in appraisal interviewing. And training appraisers in coaching skills as an extension of traditional approaches to performance appraisal training is vital.

Guidelines for Appraisal Interviewing

A summary of what are most frequently seen to be key elements in effective appraisal interviewing is set out below. These guidelines must be interpreted with caution, since a high degree of flexibility is likely to be shown by good interviewers in dealing with the widely differing problems and needs of individual employees.

Begin the interview with a clear statement of purpose.
This will help to generate a purposeful interaction, and remind both parties how the formal appraisal interview, as a key part of the performance appraisal process, can be differentiated from informal appraisal and counselling sessions.

Attempt to put the employee at ease, and establish rapport.
This process will be assisted if a high degree of mutual trust and confidence characterizes manager–employee relationships. Rapport will be more readily established if adequate informal counselling and guidance on performance is provided, so that the employee is confident that no surprise issues will be raised, and that the formal appraisal interview will be used to review achievements and problems previously discussed informally.

Discuss the main tasks and responsibilities undertaken by the employee and invite comments.
Where the employee completes a self-appraisal document, it may be useful for the appraiser to initiate the discussion by reviewing the employee's comments concerning job objectives and key tasks.

Ensure a balanced discussion takes place.
This requires not only that praise be given for good work, but also that areas of deficient performance be frankly faced up to and discussed. Where possible it is desirable that praise and criticism be related to expected standards of job performance and that comments on personal characteristics and personality traits be minimized, except in so far as these have a major impact on job performance and future potential.

Encourage the appraisee to talk freely about any frustration in the job, and about problem areas.
Probing questions asked by the appraiser assist the appraisee to identify underlying problems and to generate possible solutions.

Encourage the appraisee to develop self-analysis and self-discovery.
If the appraisers avoid a 'spoon-feeding' approach, they can attempt to encourage appraisees to think through points raised either in their self-appraisal document or in the interview discussion, to help them develop a better understanding of the areas where change and improvement is required.

Consider the year ahead, including action to develop performance.
In encouraging appraisees to talk about career expectations, appraisers can assist them to relate their ambitions to likely organizational opportunities.

Bring the interview to a close with a summary and plan for future action.
This permits both parties to clarify what action is expected of them following the interview.

Problems of Appraisal Interviewing

Although many organizations have devoted a great deal of time, effort and resources to the setting up of performance appraisal schemes, the results have often been disappointing. While there has been considerable progress in improving the instruments of performance appraisal systems, especially by shifting from the more subjective, often simplistic methods to more sophisticated, objectively based approaches, the implementation of performance appraisal still tends to be resisted, if not avoided, by many managers.

One difficulty is the face-to-face situation of the appraisal interview, where the appraiser sits down with the appraisee and reviews his or her performance. When situations are full of positives appraisal is easy, for example when performance and potential are good, when superior and subordinate have an open relationship, when promotions or salary increases are abundant, when there is plenty of time for preparation and discussion. In short, whenever it is a pleasure, performance appraisal is easy to do.

Most of the time, however, and particularly when it is most needed and most difficult to do, performance appraisal refuses to run properly. Beer (1981) suggests three main sources of difficulty:

- The quality of the relationship between appraiser and appraisee.
- The manner and skill with which the interview is conducted.
- The appraisal system itself, namely the objectives the organization expects it to achieve, the methodology, the documents and procedures that make up the system.

The underlying quality of the superior–subordinate relationship has a major impact, since the appraisal process is part of a broader set of interactions between the appraiser and appraisee. Unless there is good mutual trust and understanding, the appraisee is likely to view appraisal discussions with apprehension and suspicion. The appraiser, in turn, is likely to view appraisal time as a daunting experience where employee hostility and resistance is likely to emerge.

While the appraiser–appraisee relationship should be characterized by high levels of trust and understanding, these qualities alone are not sufficient to ensure that the underlying relationships are conducive to effective appraisals.

It is vital for informal appraisal, feedback and coaching meetings to take place on a continuing basis as and when required. The importance of the timing and specificity of feedback, in terms of giving praise to an employee at the appropriate time when a task has been done well, and of criticizing and entering into constructive but candid discussion when a mistake has been made, has been emphasized by many writers. Probably the most highly publicized advocates of this important managerial skill are the authors of the *One Minute Manager* (Blanchard and Johnson, 1983).

If regular informal appraisal takes place, the problems of hoarding up points to deal with at the appraisal interview and of springing surprises on employees should be avoided.

The appraisal interview is a most difficult type of interview for any manager to undertake. Managers often experience feelings of unease at the prospect of entering a situation with staff in which a more candid and personal set of exchanges is likely to take place than probably at any other time. In addition, the manager may be exposing himself or herself to criticism. If the interview is not well handled, the downside risks are considerable, in terms of potential damage that can be done to self-image, motivation and working relationships. Two of the major problems that may occur in an imperfectly conducted appraisal interview are avoidance and defensiveness.

Avoidance

If supervisors are uncomfortable about their organizational role in carrying out appraisal and are fearful of the consequences of being frank in conveying negative comments to staff, the major problems and issues of employee job performance are likely to be avoided. Instead, the appraiser may skate over in a vague way or indulge in a conversation about relatively superficial and trivial matters. The problem may be compounded and reinforced by the appraisee's fear of learning things that may diminish his or her self-image. Thus the appraisee may be reluctant to use opportunities in the interview to seek feedback that could have negative aspects, and will enter into an implicit collision of avoidance with the appraiser.

Defensiveness

Defensive behaviour may emerge in various forms at the appraisal interview with damaging effects. For example, a member of staff may attempt to explain away problems or poor performance by blaming others or situational factors. The appraiser, on the other hand, may be inclined to see the staff member's own qualities, failings and inadequacies as the cause of problems without fully recognizing external factors.

Defensiveness may take the form of hostility, denial or aggressive behaviour. On the other hand, the employee may enter into a submissive state outwardly acquiescent and compliant, but inwardly disagreeing and building up feelings of grievance towards the appraiser. If the interviewer is excessively judgemental, conveys a large number of negative points and fails to support negative feedback with specific evidence, defensive behaviour on the part of the appraisee damaging to the appraisal process and to longer-term relationships is likely to occur.

References

Anderson, G.C. and Barnett, J.G. 1986: Nurse appraisal in practice. *Health Service Journal*, 96, 5023.

Anderson, G.C. and Barnett, J.G. 1987: The characteristics of effective appraisal interviews. *Personnel Review*, 16 (4).

Anstey, E. and Fletcher, C.A. 1976: *Staff Appraisal and Development.* London: Walker J Allen and Unwin.

Barnett, J.G. and Anderson, G.C. 1985: *Nursing staff development programme: An enquiry into the effectiveness of the appraisal interview.* Edinburgh: Scottish Health Service Management Development Group.

Beer, M. 1981: Performance appraisal: Dilemmas and possibilities. *Organizational Dynamics*, Winter.

Blanchard, K. and Johnson, S. 1983: *The One Minute Manager.* London: Fontana/Collins.

Brinkerhoff, D.W. and Kanter, R.M. 1980: Appraising the performance of performance appraisal. *Sloan Management Review*, Spring, 3–16.

Burke, R.J., Weitzel, W. and Weir, T. 1978: Characteristics of effective employee performance review and development interviews: Replication and extension. *Personnel Psychology*, 31 (3), 903–18.

Buzzotta, V.R. and Lefton, R.E. 1979: Performance appraisal: Is it worth it? *Industrial Engineering*, January, 20–4.

Fletcher, C.A. 1978: Manager/subordinate communication and leadership style: A field study of this relationship to perceived outcomes of appraisal interviews. *Personal Review,* 7 (1), Winter.

Gill, D. 1977: *Appraising Performance* (pp. 56–60). London: IPM.

Greller, M.M. 1978: The nature of subordinate participation in the appraisal interview. *Academy of Management Journal,* 21 (4), 646–58.

Lawler, E.E., Mohrman, A.M. and Resnick-West, S.M. 1984: Performance appraisal revisited. *Organizational Dynamics,* Summer.

Long, P. 1986: *Performance Appraisal Revisited* (pp. 43–5). London: IPM.

Maier, N.R.F. 1958: *The Appraisal Interview.* New York: John Wiley.

Margerison, C. 1976: A Constructive approach to appraisal. *Personnel Management,* 8 (7), July, 30–3.

Meyer, H.H., Kay, E. and French, J.R.P. 1965: Split roles in performance appraisal. *Harvard Business Review,* 43 (1), 123–9.

Parkinson, R. 1977: Recipe for a realistic appraisal system. *Personnel Management,* 9 (11), November.

Pym, D. 1973: The politics and rituals of appraisals. *Occupational Psychology,* 47 (4).

Rothaus, P., Morton, R.B. and Hanson, P.E. 1965: Performance appraisal and psychological distance. *Journal of Applied Psychology,* 49 (1), 48–54.

Wexley, K.N., Singh, J.P. and Yukl, G.A. 1973: Subordinate personality as a moderator of the effects of participation in three types of appraisal interviews. *Journal of Applied Psychology,* 58 (1), 54–9.

9

Managing Linkages Between Performance Appraisal and Pay

A question of fundamental importance is to what extent, if at all, links should exist between performance appraisal and pay decisions. In the past, different approaches have been advocated by British and American writers, and have been reflected in different organizational practices, although there is now some evidence to suggest a shift towards more generally held views on how performance appraisal and pay should be related, even though substantial variations in organizational practice remain.

American literature has consistently articulated the merits of relating performance appraisal to pay. Lawler (1981), while generally advocating close linkages, recognizes that a number of factors will influence the feasibility and the desirability of using performance appraisals in making pay decisions. Data gathered by Peck (1984), and summarized in table 9.1, is illustrative of a number of American surveys highlighting that many American organizations use performance appraisals for pay decisions, in ensuring that those who emerge from the system of performance appraisal as high performers receive greater pay rewards than those considered to be less good performers.

The traditional British approach has been to stress the advantages of separating performance appraisal from pay decisions. This approach stresses the existence of conflict among the various objectives performance appraisal schemes could be expected to fulfil in organizations. Randell, Packard and Slater (1984) have been putting forward the argument for many years for the separation of the main

Table 9.1　Purpose of performance appraisal in 510 companies

Purpose	Number of companies (n = 510)
Determining merit increases	459
Providing basis of feedback on employees' performance	442
Planning goals for job performance with employees	401
Determining training and development needs	352
Identifying promotion potential	346
Identifying employees with specific skills and abilities	236

Source: Peck (1984, p. 20)

elements of performance appraisal into three distinct reviews for future potential, current performance and salary discussions. Randell, in keeping with a number of other British writers, considers that the objective of using performance appraisal ratings for salary decision is in conflict with other performance appraisal objectives, especially those concerned with improving current performance, and identifying the training and development needs of appraisees. Most organizations, even if agreeing to some extent with Randell, Packard and Slater's proposition in theory, reject it for practical considerations, taking the view that three separate sets of reviews would make unreasonable demands on time and resources.

Anstey, Fletcher and Walker (1976) oppose linking pay increases to performance appraisal through fear of trade union opposition: 'If trade unions suspect that the appraisal scheme is an indirect means of assessing the pay that various staff merit, they are likely to oppose the scheme – and with good reason.' Attitudes in the UK and elsewhere have undergone change since the late 1970s, and especially since the late 1980s. The concept of performance-related pay is now more widely accepted. Opposition from trade unions has not been the major impediment, as predicted by Anstey, although it has to be said, union views vary considerably on this subject. In the teaching profession in Scotland, some reluctance towards the concept of performance appraisal was expressed in 1991 by the Educational Institute of Scotland (the EIS), the union which represents primary school teachers and some secondary teachers, as performance appraisal was about to be applied for the first time to teachers in state schools in Scotland. It should be noted, however, that this opposition was towards a scheme that was unrelated to pay. In banking, union attitudes towards pay have become more positive, especially where it can be shown that staff are likely to be better off financially with performance-related pay, than without it.

Quite apart from trade union considerations, attitudes towards performance-related pay have generally become more positive. It is interesting to note signs of change even in the late 1970s. Gill (1977) states, in reviewing performance appraisal practice based on an IPM study:

> While we would advocate along with other writers and, demonstrably, the majority of our participants, that appraisals and salary reviews should be separate, it would seem both sensible and logical that the two exercises should not be too widely separated in terms of time ... one of our participants suggested that the ideal time interval was between three and six months, as this would give a chance for a below average performer to improve and thus not be penalised in salary terms.

In recent years organizations have generally been expressing greater interest in relating performance appraisal to pay. The UK Government's Advisory and Conciliation and Arbitration Service (ACAS, 1988) has noted an increased level of interest in links between reward reviews and performance assessment, although it is surprising that in the UK IPM survey of performance appraisal practice, Long (1986) reports little change in the number of responding organizations who use performance appraisals for making salary decisions – 40 per cent compared with 39 per cent in the previous similar, broadly based survey some nine years earlier. When the UK IPM next conducts a survey, it is extremely likely that the number of organizations linking performance appraisal to salary decisions will be very much higher.

Managing performance appraisal systems to drive pay and reward decisions can have a major impact on the effectiveness of any organization, through influencing the motivation of employees, the recruitment and retention of high-calibre staff, and the culture of the organization. Lawler (1981) puts forward evidence to support the proposition that when performance appraisal is linked to pay and reward decisions, employees are motivated to perform more effectively. In addition organizations find it easier to recruit and retain high-performing staff, and develop performance-oriented cultures. While organizations can develop other strategies to bring about these desirable outcomes regarding human resources, a well-designed and well-managed performance appraisal system linked to pay and rewards can make a major contribution to these other goals of HRM.

Performance appraisal systems linked to pay decisions will work more effectively under certain organization conditions. It should be noted that the process is two-way, and that not only can performance appraisal drive pay decisions, but the linkages with pay can also affect performance appraisal, in both positive and negative ways.

What, then, are these positive and negative considerations?

On the positive side, if performance appraisal and pay are linked:

- All parties concerned take performance appraisal more seriously.
- Many individuals view this as the fairest basis for pay awards, according to research evidence (e.g. Prince and Lawler, 1986).
- A performance-oriented culture develops, where it becomes accepted that high performers receive greater rewards, and low performers receive poorer rewards.

On the negative side:

- The pay issue may overshadow other performance appraisal issues, e.g. issues concerned with training and development.
- Individuals may be inclined to set lower goals than they are capable of achieving.
- Appraisers may feel under pressure to give high ratings.
- Appraisal discussions may become less open and honest.

Conditions for Effective Appraisal/Pay Linkages

A number of factors will influence the extent to which it is feasible and desirable to link the performance appraisal system to pay decisions.

Job design Unless jobs are designed in ways that allow individual performance to be clearly assessed, it will be difficult to create an effective linkage to pay decisions. In highly interactive job situations, pay could be more fairly determined on a group basis.

Open effective communications Without this, it is unlikely a performance appraisal scheme can be operated that will lead to valid conclusions about the performance of staff.

High level of interpersonal and appraisal skills Appraisers require the skills and confidence to carry out honest and effective appraisals, emphasizing constructive discussion as far as possible.

Sound appraisal design The appraisal scheme must be carefully designed, with the pay linkage in mind. For example, careful thought must be given to the number of rating scale points for overall ratings.

Supportive organizational culture The culture needs to be one in which doing performance appraisal well is valued, and in which relating appraisal to pay is considered legitimate.

In effect linkages to pay decisions put extra pressures on any system of performance appraisal. For pay decisions to be considered fair and legitimate when determined on this basis, it is crucially important that the performance appraisal system has been soundly designed and carefully implemented leading to valid overall performance ratings.

Case Studies

The current experiences of two organizations – the first in the transportation field, the second a major bank – are summarized below.

Organization A: Transportation company

The performance appraisal scheme includes overall ratings on a five point scale (one is high, five is low), although the middle point, at the request of managers, have been subdivided into 3(i) and 3(ii). Formerly, precise pay percentage figures were tied to each rating – with a five rating earning a zero pay increase, a four rating the standard cost-of-living only, a three rating the cost-of-living plus a fixed percentage, two and one ratings earning the cost-of-living plus successively higher percentage increases. One aspect of this approach (now discontinued) was that people had a clear idea what they would be getting, once their performance appraisal ratings were established. This company has operated an open appraisal scheme for over five years; the linkages with pay have applied only to managers.

The company now operates a more complex system where the pay increase for managers is still linked, to some extent, through the mechanism just described, but other factors now enter into the final decision on how large a pay increase a manager receives, namely:

their position in their grade, and a discretionary element determined normally by the reviewer or 'grandfather' figure. If, for example, two individuals both receive a two rating, the person who is lower in the grade would be eligible for a greater pay increase than the person more highly positioned in the grade. After performance appraisal ratings are determined, and signed off by the reviewer, they are submitted to the central personnel function, which will process the data and send it back to the reviewer, showing pay eligibility bands for each of the managers who have been appraised, the calculations being based on grade position and performance appraisal ratings. The reviewer can use discretion, on a limited basis, in determining the precise pay increase for each manager.

In summary, the present policy for determining managers' pay depends on:

- overall performance appraised ratings, using a five-point scale
- present salary position within grade
- discretionary element determined by the reviewer or 'grandfather' and confirmed by the 'great grandfather'.

One of the main reasons for the change from the former, simpler system of a direct appraisal to pay linkage, to the more complex present system, was that many managers had reached, or were about to reach, their grade maximum. The change of policy was accompanied by an extension upwards of grade maximum points, to roughly the mid-point of the grade above, to permit more flexibility and give greater opportunity to reward the high performers.

A key issue is clearly the validity of overall ratings, and the extent to which they are skewed towards the upper end of the scale.

Two approaches used by this organization to minimize the problem of high ratings, linked to higher pay awards than can reasonably be justified are:

1. Active reviewing by the 'grandfather' figure. For example the reviewer may call a meeting of his direct reports who are appraisers after a round of appraisals, to examine the consistency and fairness of the ratings made of their staff.
2. A scaling down of the actual amount of money linked to the higher ratings, the greater the number of individuals who receive a 'one' or 'two' rating.

This is analogous to the football pools principle of scaling down first dividends, the larger number of winners. The present system of linking performance appraisal and pay for managers in a direct, but not totally mechanistic way, appears to be working reasonably well. One aspect, however, is that individuals do not know what pay increase to expect, even though they are fully aware of their performance appraisal ratings.

Organization B: A major bank

This bank operates a system for its managerial employees which links performance appraisal directly with pay. The bank is now extending this scheme downwards to include those at assistant manager and branch accountant level. It is not felt it would be appropriate to push it further down the organization to clerical levels – although they are covered by formal performance appraisal.

The bank operates overall performance appraisal rating scales from one to ten, although effectively from one to eight as no one receives a nine or ten. 'One' or 'two' ratings describes performance that fails to meet expectations; ratings three, four, five and six indicate varying levels of meeting expectations, while seven and eight ratings exceed expectations.

Appraisers submit a forecast of likely appraisal ratings in advance of carrying out appraisals, to central personnel, so that salary implications can be assessed. Justifications are required for any ratings of six or above. Feedback is then provided to any departments that appear to be out of line before appraisals are carried out. It is felt, however, that there has been a slight problem in the inflation of ratings at the most senior levels, but that this problem has largely been minimized at other levels.

Pay increases are directly linked to appraisal ratings; the precise percentages are not announced till after appraisals take place. In 1990 pay awards were made on the following basis:

Appraisal ratings	Pay increase (%)
1	0.0
2	0.0
3	7.5
4	10.5
5	11.5
6	12.5
7	13.5
8	15.0

In addition, managers receive a company bonus, which is weighted by appraisal ratings, so that high performers receive a bigger company bonus than low performers. The system seems to operate reasonably well; one problem identified is that objectives set within the appraisal scheme are not as sharply defined, or as challenging as they should be.

The Options in Determining Performance Appraisal and Pay Linkages

Broadly, three main options are available, as outlined below.

The direct-linking approach The advantages of the direct linking approach are:

Strong management control: The decision on the nature of the linkage can be made at a very senior level, and implemented without delays involving other decision-making processes.

Avoids relativity/potential grievance problems among departments: All those evaluated at the same performance level receive the same percentage merit increase.

Adds credibility to the performance appraisal scheme: It is seen as having important, direct financial implications.

The problems and issues are likely to be:

Need to avoid upward inflation of performance appraisal ratings: This can be helped through active participation by those in the 'grandfather' roles.

The development of linkages that are seen to be fair and reasonable: These should aid the motivation of managers, if worked out carefully on a sound basis.

Need to avoid pay issues overshadowing all other aspects of performance appraisal: This implies the need for some separation in time between the appraisal interview and the payment decision.

Discretionary pay increases have the advantage of:

• involving appraisers and reviewers actively in the decision-making process re merit pay
• providing flexibility in the system
• giving managers the opportunity to improve their performance after appraisal interviews, and have this reflected in higher pay increases – potential difficulties include possible disparities and perceived unfairness

in the way the system of payments is implemented through decentralized managerial discretion.

The intermediate option of limited managerial discretion, with performance appraisal ratings being linked to ranges of values of merit pay, has most of the advantages and few of the disadvantages of the other two options identified above.

Other Matters for Consideration

Need for objectivity and consistency

Organizations which operate performance-related pay schemes need to place considerable emphasis in ensuring that their performance appraisal schemes are producing objective and consistent evaluations that are seen to be fair. This implies a number of steps that have to be taken, for example, training of appraisers; use of reviewers; monitoring studies by the personnel department, etc.

Relating pay to the achievement of objectives or to overall performance appraisal ratings

Most organizations appear to use overall performance appraisal ratings. The rationale would appear to be that while objectives are important, other aspects are too, hence the use of overall ratings. The National Westminster Bank, for example, attempts to link the achievement of objectives directly to merit pay. Its system includes in the performance appraisal scheme:

- Objectives (the aims of the job).
- Targets (the specific targets to aim at).
- Measures (how performance will be measured).
- Weightings (the relative importance of the objectives).

These factors are as specific and measurable as possible; if circumstances change during the year they can be reset.

The system includes four levels of achievement:

1. Below 'threshold' – no bonus.
2. 'Threshold' – the lowest level of achievement to justify a minimum bonus.
3. 'On-target' – the achievement of stretching but realistic targets.
4. 'Ceiling' – level of performance justifying the maximum bonus.

Problems with salary structures

Performance-related payment systems have led to overcrowding problems at the top of the salary ranges, as some individuals may reach the top of their pay range quickly. Some organizations (e.g. Cable & Wireless) have abandoned fixed pay ranges, others (e.g. National Westminster Bank) have reduced their number of salary scales while extending the range of each one.

Culture changes

Many commentators (e.g. IDS, 1990) have drawn attention to the fact that performance appraisal/merit pay system, as well as reflecting organization culture, can be a powerful agent for bringing about cultural change, with far-reaching implications for the organization, its employees and the extent to which they experience satisfaction with their jobs, and with the organization.

Summary

Linking performance appraisal helps the credibility and sustainability of performance appraisal, as well as providing a sound basis for pay decisions and a performance-oriented culture. As has been shown, a number of issues must be addressed, the most important of which are:

- The nature and numbers of employees included.
- The nature of job design.
- Monitoring the appraisal scheme to avoid the inflation of ratings.
- Above all, the soundness of the design and implementation of the performance appraisal scheme.

References

ACAS 1988: Advisory Booklet No. 11, *Employee Appraisal.*
Anstey, E., Fletcher, C. and Walker, J. 1976: *Staff Appraisal and Development.* London: Allen and Unwin.
Gill, D. 1977: *Appraising Performance.* London: IPM.
IDS (Income Data Services) 1990: *Putting Pay Philosophies Into Practice.* July.

Lawler, E.E. 1981: *Pay and Organisational Development.* Reading, Mass.: Addison Wesley.

Long, P. 1986: *Performance Appraisal Revisited.* London: IPM.

Peck, C.A. 1984: Pay and performance: The interaction of compensation and performance appraisal. Research Bulletin No. 155. New York. Conference Board.

Prince, J.B. and Lawler, E.E. 1986: Does salary discussion hurt the developmental performance appraisal? *Organisational Behaviour and Human Decision Processes,* 37.

Randell, G.A., Packard, P.M.A. and Slater, A.J. 1984: *Staff Appraisal: A First Step to Effective Leadership* 3rd Edn. London: IPM.

10

Managing the Relationship of Performance Appraisal and Career Development

As previously discussed, effective, sustainable systems of performance appraisal place emphasis on future-oriented, developmental objectives. Developmental objectives which a system of performance appraisal can attempt to pursue include:

- The identification of training and development needs.
- The agreement on a range of actions to develop the appraisee, and to improve performance.
- Clarification of career paths and career opportunities available to the appraisee.
- Counselling on career issues, relating the appraisee's skills, abilities, attitudes and values to possible future jobs.

The inclusion of discussion about career development issues can have a positive impact on appraisal interviews in a number of ways:

- The line manager (assuming the immediate line manager is the appraiser) is seen as taking an active interest in the careers of employees, and is not focusing only on short-term performance improvement. Employees find it motivating and encouraging to discover their line managers are interested in their careers.
- Discussions in this area remind line managers they have, or should have, certain responsibilities in enhancing the career development of their staff.
- Information and advice about career paths provide a medium and long-term context for employees in which to operate, and shall assist in motivating them by clarifying career goals they can seek to attain.

- Because of the speed of change in organizations and in the environments in which they operate, all employees derive benefit from a periodic update about their career opportunities.

In addition, data included on performance appraisal documentation summarizing the conclusions and actions agreed regarding career developments issues can be incorporated into a career management and succession planning system as part of an integrated approach to HRM.

Conditions for Establishing an Effective Link Between Performance Appraisal and Career Development

A number of conditions must be established if performance appraisal is to make an effective contribution to issues relating to the career development of employees.

Evaluation of potential

Although some writers (e.g. Randell, Packard and Slater, 1984) have advocated the separation of performance appraisal and the evaluation of the future potential of employees, survey evidence (Long, 1986) suggests that the practice in many organizations is to combine the processes. Yet the trend that emerges in the UK, based on data gathered by the IPM (Gill, 1977; Long, 1986), shows some reduction in the number of companies including the evaluation of employee potential as one of the objectives of their performance appraisal systems, even though many organizations – 71 per cent of the large sample of companies included in the 1986 survey – identify this as an objective for their systems of performance appraisal. This data is presented in chapter 2 and the reasons for the downward trend, given that 87 per cent of organizations in the earlier 1977 survey had identified the evaluation of potential as an appraisal purpose, are discussed in some detail in that chapter. These reasons can be summarized as dissatisfaction with simple, subjective ways of assessing the potential of employees, slow economic growth in the UK at the time of the surveys, the shift towards flatter, less hierarchical organizations and the emergence of new methods, especially assessment centres, for identifying and evaluating the future potential of employees.

Clearly, there can be difficulties in asking line managers to evaluate the future potential rather than the current performance of their staff. Some of these difficulties have been well documented, e.g. by Woodruffe (1990), who points out that line managers will often be idiosyncratic in their ratings and focus on those competency dimensions that they value personally. Personal likes and dislikes will affect assessments. Other problems are that the line managers will often have a limited vision of the precise nature of higher level jobs, and their competency requirements.

Woodruffe strongly advocates that performance appraisal should be regarded as an alternative to assessment centres, but others think it should be considered an additional mechanism and an opportunity for making an assessment of the future potential of employees. While recognizing the limitations of the line manager's perspective, the closeness of the working relationship with staff suggests that his or her view of their potential should at least be taken into account and incorporated in a performance appraisal system, although there are good arguments for using other approaches such as assessment centres in addition.

Lawler, Mohrman and Resnick-West's (1984) view differs from Randell, Packard and Slater's (1984) in that they recommend an integrated approach to performance appraisal, rather than holding totally separate reviews for current performance, future potential and the determination of rewards, on the grounds of administrative simplicity and less time evolved. Nevertheless, such separation in time within an integrated performance appraisal system of the elements concerned with the assessment of current performance and the evaluation of future potential can be achieved. Such an approach is illustrated in chapter 13, in the case study on the system of performance appraisal in Scottish Nuclear Ltd.

The use of assessment centres

While a full consideration of this subject lies outside the scope of this book, I am firmly of the belief that the use of assessment centres, making available the data that emerges about employees' competencies and development needs, can enhance the understanding and insights of both appraisers and appraisees into appraisal and career development issues.

While the term 'assessment centre' is open to different interpretations, a commonly used definition is the 'assessment of a group of individuals by a team of judges using a comprehensive and integrated series of techniques' (Fletcher, 1982). Originally assessment centres were used primarily for selection purposes, but increasingly they are used for the purpose of identifying training and development needs, and future potential.

While the format and design will vary according to the requirements of the particular organization, an effective assessment centre should normally include the following:

- a variety of assessment techniques
- several (usually six to eight) candidates
- several assessors/observers
- assessments resulting from a number of individual and group activities, organized into a grid, which relates competencies to roles required for effective job performance. (See figure 10.1, which is broadly typical of the approach used in many assessment centres, linking competencies with various job roles.)

Dissemination of information about careers and career paths

For performance appraisal to be linked effectively to career development, appraisers and appraisees should be fully briefed on the organization's philosophy towards career development and career paths. In addition, it is highly desirable that appraisers and appraisees should receive training on theories and principles relating to careers, to increase their understanding and their ability to participate effectively in interview discussions on the subject. For example, it is helpful if they have an appreciation of the concept of 'career anchors' described later in this chapter.

Career counselling skills

Appraisers should receive training in counselling skills to assist them in conducting what can often be an extremely difficult and sensitive part of the appraisal interview. Further, these skills will need to be used, as part of the management process, whenever an employee seeks advice on career issues outside the formal performance appraisal system.

In addition, human resource specialists should be available to provide advice on career issues that lie beyond the capability of the line manager.

Figure 10.1 Assessment centre design

Competency Exercise/Activity	A Self-Confidence	B Incisiveness	C Breadth of Vision	D Initiative	E Sensitivity to needs of others	F Persistence
1. In basket	x	x	x			
2. Presentation	x		x	x	x	
3. Creative thinking exercise	x		x			
4. Group negotiating exercise	x	x	x	x	x	x
5. Financial exercise		x	x			x
6. Influencing exercise	x			x	x	x

For productive discussions to take place on the career development of the individual, both at the appraisal interview, and in less formal situations as appropriate throughout the year, it is important that both appraisers and appraisees should have awareness of a number of career development concepts. While a full discussion of career development lies beyond the scope of this book, a particularly relevant concept to performance appraisal discussions is that of career anchors.

Career Anchors

This concept was formulated by Schein (1975), and emerged from the results of a longitudinal study of graduates from an American higher educational institution (the Sloan School) in which he interviewed these graduates some ten or twelve years into their careers and explored with them their reasons for career and job choice. Although participants in this study felt they were often making short-term adjustments to their careers, longer-term patterns were emerging, giving rise to the concept of 'career anchors' which help to explain how a person's career develops. Schein's concept of career anchors refers to a concept held by individuals about themselves, and which evolves and is adjusted through experience. There are three components to the career anchor concept:

1. Self-perceived skills and abilities (based on perceived successes and failures in different work situations).
2. Self-perceived motives and needs (based on self-diagnosis resulting from experience in different work settings, and on feedback from others).
3. Self-perceived attitudes and values (based on encounters between the individual and the values and norms of employing organizations).

The career anchor concept represents a set of inner forces within the individual which have a driving, a constraining and a stabilizing influence on the consideration of career development and career options.

Schein (1978) identifies a number of categories of career anchors as outlined below.

Technical functional competence   People in this category place most emphasis in making career choices on the technical and functional content of jobs. Individuals who are strongly rooted in this area of career anchors will often feel very insecure about moving out of their technical or functional specialization. People with this inclination may prefer to leave companies rather than be promoted to a managerial position.

Managerial competence Those in this category can be expected to be strongly motivated to attain managerial posts. Technical or functional jobs are seen as a means to an end – the end being managerial work in which the individuals in this group view themselves as possessing competencies.

Security and stability Security can be an important force influencing the career decisions of some people, in a number of ways. People in this category may be driven by strong feelings about job security in making career choices; in other cases security is geographically based with emphasis on restricting career moves within a particular geographical area; another manifestation is in seeking stability in the family, and in attempting to achieve integration within a community.

Creativity This category of career anchor is typified by the entrepreneur. Some people have a primary need to build or create something that is entirely or largely their own product. People driven by this career anchor are likely to get bored quickly by routine jobs, and are primarily influenced in making career choices by the search for new challenges.

Autonomy and independence People in this group have often found organizational life to be restrictive, and may be inclined to develop their careers by leaving large organizations and setting up business on their own. Sometimes this career anchor may be easy to confuse with that of the entrepreneurs who are in the creative category, since entrepreneurs also enjoy freedom and autonomy if they are successful. The differentiating factor is that while entrepreneurs are motivated in career terms to create something – usually a product and a market – those in the autonomy category are influenced largely in critical choices by the need for freedom and the opportunity to develop their own distinctive life styles.

Basis identity This anchor applies to people whose main career satisfaction is derived from achieving and sustaining membership of a particular occupation or profession. In the case of some occupational groups, title, uniform and symbols associated with the job all contribute strongly to self-image and career identity.

Service to others For some, the factors influencing career decisions relate to the provision of service to others. Those who come within this category are likely to seek careers in, for example, social work or, teaching.

Power, influence and control Schein indicates that he is not totally certain that needs for power are a separate career anchor, although he considers that some individuals (e.g. politicians) come within this category.

Variety The driving force for some individuals in making decisions about jobs and careers is the need for variety. This anchor is likely to apply to people with a range of talents, who feel bored or concerned at the prospect of utilizing and developing only some of their abilities.

For appraisers and appraisees, an awareness of the concept of career anchors and the different categories will make discussions about the career aspirations and career development of the individual more productive by:

- assisting individuals in self-diagnosis of their own motives and values relating to careers
- creating an understanding of the range of different approaches towards career choices
- highlighting patterns of consistency in the way careers evolve
- providing clearer awareness of forces that have influenced career decisions in the past, when decisions about future career issues have to be made.

Instruments have been designed by Schein and Delong (1981) and others to help people find out their own primary career anchors. Such instruments can form a useful element in a training programme on career management or on the relationship between performance appraisal and career management.

The career anchor concept is of considerable practical value in classifying career types, and in providing insight into different personal attitudes and values towards careers. This can be particularly valuable in appraisal interviews where appraiser and appraisee have widely differing value systems on careers. The career anchor concept, and its various categories, helps to identify the basis for different viewpoints, and contributes to better mutual understanding in discussing career issues.

Schein (1978) points out that career anchors reflect the underlying needs and motives which an individual brings into working life. They also reflect the individual's values and discovered talents. According to Schein' the concept describes the process of 'integrating into the total self-concept what one sees oneself to be more or less competent at, wanting out of life, one's value system and the kind of person one is that begins to determine the major life and occupational choices throughout adulthood'.

Other career concepts that appraisers and appraisees should be aware of include career structures or career ladders. These terms can be used interchangeably. Career structures or ladders (referred to from now onwards as career ladders for reasons of simplifying the terminology) should contain two or more steps clarifying how individuals can progress their careers in a given direction – whether manual, clerical, technical, professional, functional or managerial – in an organization. An illustration of the career ladder for secretaries in a British university is shown in appendix 10.1.

A sound career ladder should consist of several, progressive steps, each showing a requirement for the ability, skills and experience to perform work of growing complexity, responsibility and importance. Career ladders should be published, and all relevant staff should be given access to this information. As far as possible clear criteria should be laid down for each rung on a career ladder. Information of this type provides an objective foundation for the discussion of an individual's career at an appraisal interview. How a person moves upwards in a career ladder depends on both the design of the organization's structure and the extent to which jobs can be flexibly defined. Broadly, two paths can be followed. Either the individual progresses through promotion to a higher level in the organizational hierarchy or through a redefinition and expansion of their present job. Both options can apply in the case of university secretaries in Britain, as illustrated in appendix 10.1.

Handy (1989) and others writing on the changing nature of organizations have highlighted the trend towards flatter, less hierarchical structures with fewer levels, to cope with the increasing pace of change. This suggests that career ladders will become increasingly linked to the expansion and enrichment of jobs and less to promotions within the organization.

Conventional organizations with a pyramid shape generally give managerial positions the highest levels of recognition towards the top of the pyramid. Mayo (1991) draws attention to the need to accept personal growth within the job as an increasingly realistic form of career development in the future.

There is a danger that if excessive emphasis is placed on career development issues, problems will result. Handy (1985), for example, draws attention to the dangers of confusing promises with plans, given the organizational uncertainties within which career planning takes place. He cites the example of an organization in which only 10 per cent of the managers involved in a career management scheme were in the positions planned for them ten years before; 35 per cent of the managers had left the organization entirely.

Future unpredictabilities, however, do not negate the value of attempting to develop effective links between performance appraisal and career development – which are beneficial, as noted at the beginning of this chapter – to individuals and the organization.

References

Fletcher, C.A. 1982: Assessment centres. In D.M. Davey and M. Harris (eds), *Judging People*. London: McGraw-Hill.

Gill, D. 1977: *Appraising Performance*. London: IPM.

Handy, C. 1985: *Understanding Organisations* 3rd edn. London: Penguin.

Handy, C. 1989: *The Age of Unreason*. London: Business Books.

Lawler, E.E., Mohrman, A.M. and Resnick-West, S.M. 1984: Performance appraisal revisited, *Organisational Dynamics*, Summer.

Long, P. 1986: *Performance Appraisal Revisited*. London: IPM.

Mayo, A. 1991: *Managing Careers: Strategies for Organisations*. London: IPM.

Randell, G.A., Packard, P.M.A. and Slater, A.J. 1984: *Staff Appraisal: A First Step to Effective Leadership* 3rd edn. London: IPM.

Schein, E.H. 1975: How 'career anchors' hold executives to their career paths. *Personnel*, 52 (3).

Schein, E.H. 1978: *Career Dynamics: Matching Individual and Organisational Needs*. Reading, Mass.: Addison Wesley.

Schein, E.H. and Delong, T.J. 1981: *Career Orientations Questionnaire*. Boston, Mass.: MIT.

Woodruffe, C. 1990: *Assessment Centres: Identifying and Developing Competence*. London: IPM. 1990.

Appendix 10.1

University of Strathclyde

Secretarial, Clerical and Related Staff

Revised Grade Definitions

Grade 1

Routine work involving well-defined procedures under regular or direct supervision. The tasks carried out will normally be of a repetitive nature, allowing little scope for the exercise of personal initiative. This grade should also be regarded as an entry and training grade. It is expected that an employee under training will not spend more than one year in this grade, subject to satisfactory service.

Grade 2

Work along specified lines but requiring some experience, personal responsibility and initiative. Work to daily routine but will have certain amount of responsibility for dealing with matters without close supervision. General clerical duties may involve the checking and overseeing of work of Grade 1 staff or the exercise of more advanced audio/shorthand typing skills and more complex copy typing.

Grade 3

Work requiring the exercise of considerable personal responsibility, judgement and initiative although still subject to overall well-defined limits either requiring detailed knowledge of a particular branch of work not necessarily to a standard for which a professional qualification might be appropriate or work of a supervisory nature where number of persons supervised is limited (e.g. between two and four) and the type of work is routine. Independence in the arrangement of own work, a variation in the daily schedule and under minimum of supervisory control would be the main features of work to be found in this grade.

Grade 4

Special responsibility requiring the exercise of initiative to decide on courses of action, for a clearly defined section or sub-section of work. Work will either be mainly of a supervisory nature where persons supervised are engaged on different aspects of the same work and/or large numbers involved (e.g. between five and ten) or will demand the application of specialist knowledge or will have a mainly organizational content requiring a relatively high degree of personal initiative and responsibility.

Grade 5

(a) Job content will involve the deployment of assigned resources towards defined objectives and, within defined limits, accountability for the outcome;
   or
   involve decisions which require a knowledge of general principles and standard practices in technical, financial, semi-professional or similar fields;
   or
   executive decisions which require a knowledge of the relevant broad policies or rules of the institution.
   [*NOTE*: Some jobs may involve elements of all three]
(b) Post-holders exercise a high level of personal responsibility and initiative and possess expertise and specialized knowledge, coupled with

appropriate relevant experience and/or qualifications (not necessarily of a professional standard).

Grade 6

Job content will be similar in character to posts in Grade 5 but the responsibility level will be more demanding. Within the delegated area of authority of the post job-holders will be expected to exercise responsibility at the overall level characterized below. The duties and responsibilities are examples; they are not intended for use as a comprehensive list each of which has to be undertaken to qualify for entry into this grade.

- Determining objectives to be achieved within existing policies and resources.
- Setting and monitoring standards, authorizing substantial transactions and resolving problems involving other departments or clients or contractors.
- Advising on and proposing changes in policies, plans, priorities and office systems.
- Selecting, or playing a major part in the selection of staff, and managing them.

11

Integrating Performance Appraisal with Coaching, Counselling and Mentoring

Integrating performance appraisal with coaching, counselling and mentoring has been to a large extent neglected, both in practice and in the literature. A growing number of writers, however (e.g. Novarra, 1986), are suggesting that, in terms of achieving improvements in employee performance, this is an area that requires greater attention. This view is reinforced by the increasing emphasis in a number of organizations being placed on the development objectives associated with the setting of goals, identifying and meeting training needs and helping individuals to develop their potential.

Increasingly the literature has been stressing that effective performance appraisal is not a set of periodic, discrete evaluations of employee performance, but rather a system which impacts favourably on day-to-day work performance. The concept of performance management has recently emerged in the literature (e.g. Neale, 1991) stressing the need for feedback on performance and discussions on performance improvement and employee development to take place on a regular basis between managers and their staff, as and when the need is seen to occur, and not to be confined to formal performance appraisal discussions.

Coaching is a joint process in which manager and employee work together to find solutions to present work problems. Coaching is also an important approach in developing the capability and confidence of staff. Counselling, by contrast, involves deliberation on a wide range of issues many of which extend beyond the job into, for example, personal matters, career development etc.

Coaching as part of the manager's job is similar to coaching in sports. It is not concerned with, for example, organized training programmes: it is concerned with the informal help/guidance/training that a manager may, and should, provide to staff on a regular basis.

As pointed out by Allison (1991) coaching is work related and problem centred, while counselling is more about the employee, and the employee's feelings. Coaching is usually more open and public than counselling, which is more likely to involve confidential issues. The coaching role has no boundaries for the manager as it is an inherent part of good management practice, while there are limitations to the manager's involvement in counselling, since it may be necessary to call upon professional counselling services to deal with some problems outside the province of the manager.

Coaching does not imply leaving staff to learn merely from mistakes and pick things up by chance as they go along – it does imply a planned approach, which involves setting learning objectives. This means that a manager and member of staff should agree on:

- the knowledge and skill level the member of staff requires or should aspire to
- the present knowledge and skill possessed by that person
- a plan to bridge the gap by specifying as accurately as possible what extra knowledge and skill he or she needs to gain.

Coaching is important because it contributes to performance improvement, and it develops the knowledge and skills of the individual.

Mumford (1985) has stated that most management development occurs on the job through a variety of unstructured and often accidental processes. In his view, new features in management development are primarily concerned with the more individual processes for developing managers. In this respect, coaching is an extremely important, though often neglected and undervalued element of management development.

The Links between Coaching and Performance Appraisal

Whereas performance appraisal is a formalized system that takes place at regular – usually twelve-month – intervals, coaching is an ongoing process that should characterize day-to-day relationships between managers and their staff. Research evidence suggests that the greater the quantity and quality of coaching that takes place between a manager and his or her staff, the greater the likelihood that the formal appraisal sessions will be perceived as productive by both parties.

Coaching is also highly relevant to the setting and achievement of goals which we have previously described as an integral part of management. Again there is evidence to suggest that the coaching of staff increases the likelihood of their achieving the goals they have committed themselves to undertake.

Beer (1981) points out that an important skill for the appraiser is to develop a climate of relationships that helps employees to avoid defensive behaviour, when they try to explain away lack of progress towards the attainment of their goals by blaming others or uncontrollable events. Employees may be inclined to avoid facing up to their inability to overcome problems that are impeding their achievement of goals through fear of learning things that will diminish their self-image, often leading to a lack of initiative in being willing to face up to negative feedback. The manager requires, therefore, to be proactive in exercising a high level of interpersonal, monitoring and coaching skills in both identifying ongoing problems and periodically providing support and encouragement for employees to move towards their goals.

Establishing the right climate for coaching

Every company has its own distinctive 'climate' and many organizations strive to maintain standards of behaviour and service through a dominant corporate climate or culture, which is transmitted through coaching, counselling, mentoring and appraisal to successive generations of managers and their staff. Within an organization, however, every manager has some level of influence in creating the climate that exists within his or her own section or department.

A manager's personal style influences the climate in two ways: (1) through the 'support' elements (the level of help given to staff; the degree to which mistakes are tolerated; the extent to which staff are encouraged to experiment and try out new things); (2) through the 'pressure' elements (getting staff to commit themselves to demanding targets; expecting staff to accept change and adapt to change). Establishing a sound balance between the support and pressure elements means that managers have a people-oriented but by no means soft approach to their staff. Managers are willing to help, and invest in staff (for example, by ensuring that they receive proper training) but expect them to perform to high standards. This is the kind of climate in which coaching is likely to work effectively.

Organization climate has received attention from many authors, and has probably been most highly publicized through the writings of Peters and Waterman (1982) and others associated with the 'excellence' theme. While Peters and Waterman stressed the relevance of a positive organizational climate to corporate success, it is equally relevant to successful coaching, especially when it is recognized that there are many 'micro-climates', within the overall climate of the organization.

Effective delegation

Skilful delegation is an important aspect of coaching. Delegation is not simply a question of giving instructions, it involves entrusting staff with some authority to act and with some discretion to make decisions, within guidelines that you should clearly lay down. Skills in delegation involve sound decisions by you in terms of what to delegate, to whom, and when.

Clearly, there are risks in delegation. A member of staff will, with delegated authority, have greater discretion than before. Periodic review with you should help to minimize the risk. On a positive note, delegation also implies showing trust and confidence in the ability of staff to handle new responsibilities.

Another important skill in coaching concerns your ability to identify good opportunities to coach staff, while coping with work demands. Changes in organization, procedures, work assignments etc., are excellent coaching opportunities. Ensure you give real and important work assignments, not 'phoney' jobs, and use 'special' jobs which have to be done occasionally.

In coaching staff it is important to remember that learning is most effective when:

- individuals can see the relevance and value of what they are doing to the job
- the process is active, not passive
- the coach builds on strengths and experience
- individuals can see progress being made
- there is regular dialogue between those involved in the coaching process

- regular feedback is provided
- the coach listens carefully and comments constructively
- the coach is prepared to learn from staff!

Lastly, managers should be prepared to devote time to coaching even though they are busy, and should persist with their coaching role even when other pressures make it easy to abandon coaching.

Learning Styles

Important points to remember about the way people learn are:

- No two people learn in exactly the same way – we all learn at different speeds, and encounter different types of learning barrier.
- Learning often occurs in rapid bursts, interspersed by plateau periods when little improvement appears to take place.

In coaching staff, managers must recognize the need for an individualized approach, and appreciate that the more they understand the capabilities and limitations of their staff, the more likely they are to be able to develop effective coaching activities.

Overcoming learning barriers

Knowles (1975) has commented that a major difficulty is that many adults are ignorant of their own learning processes, and how they learn effectively. Halson (1990) stresses that a major challenge for managers, especially in organizations facing the pressures of change, is to individualize learning in practical ways through good coaching, recognizing that every employee has a unique pattern of experience that forms the foundation for further learning, performance improvement and personal development.

Paul Temporal (1982) has identified a number of learning blocks or barriers which may impede the effectiveness process of coaching and the process of development. He suggests these barriers fall into two clusters: individual and environmental. Temporal lists five individual and one environmental barrier (shown in table 11.1), and examines them with regard to the coaching process by showing:

- The effect on the learning process.
- The effect on the manager as a learner.
- The effect on the manager as a coach.

Table 11.1 Barriers to effective coaching

Nature of block to learning	Effect on a manager's learning in general	Effect on a manager-learner in the coaching situation	Effect on a manager-coach in the coaching situation
Perceptual	Manager has limited vision regarding the total range of learning sources and processes available.	Manager does not perceive the need to be coached, or similarly to assist colleagues.	The coach cannot identify the individual's real development needs and so selects the wrong tasks.
Cultural	The manager's background is such that he or she wants sources of learning to be planned.	Managers reject the idea of coaching because they have been taught to help themselves – the entrepreneurial approach.	The manager new to coaching cannot resist the temptation to give a straight answer when the learner comes with a question or problem.
Emotional/ motivational	Manager avoids entering into learning situations that are potentially painful, and that might threaten his or her security/ credibility.	Manager is reluctant to expose weaknesses to others in the organization.	The coach feels unable to share own problems, and so prevents the learner from seeing the bigger picture.
Intellectual	Manager does not believe learning to be an ongoing activity.	Manager cannot apply to other situations what he or she has learnt from his or her coaching experience.	The coach denies the need to give the learner plenty of feedback on both good and bad results.
Expressive	Because of poor listening/speaking skills, the manager underrates the value of group discussions, meetings, etc., and so avoids them.	Manager cannot clearly explain ideas, feelings, etc. to colleagues and coach.	The coach cannot translate ideas into terms and languages which are readily understandable by the learner.
Environmental (Climate)	Risk-taking is not encouraged, and so the manager does not experiment with new ideas and behaviours.	The climate is such that a manager does not feel able to be honest and open about problems feelings, etc.	The pressures from top management are such that the coach consistently checks up on how the learner is dealing with a problem/situation.

Source: Temporal (1982)

Counselling

Counselling has been defined as involving deliberation on a wide range of issues, many of which extend beyond the job into, for example, personal matters, career development etc.

Although coaching is a more obvious developmental activity involving a manager and members of staff, counselling, too, has a part to play in encouraging the development of employees.

Braithwaite and Owen (1989), two experienced practitioners of counselling in the UK, have suggested that the term 'counselling' can easily be misunderstood: 'Counselling can all too easily smack of psycho-babble; it can be seen by some as wet and defensive, or even self-indulgent, and somehow out of tune with today's dynamic, flexible, organic turbulent "Performance Culture".'

Nevertheless, given the expense of replacing people who leave, and the need to achieve ever-increasing performance from all parts of the workforce, counselling is a skill which managers will need in helping the development of managers of the future.

The essential skills of counselling are concerned with helping people to help themselves: in the processes of identifying problems, facilitating the exploration of solutions, and encouraging them to draw on their inner resources.

Counselling is particularly relevant in terms of encouraging self-development. It should be non-directive and non-judgemental. Self-directed changes are more likely to be accompanied by strong personal commitment. Farnsworth (1979) stresses that individuals must accept some of the responsibility for their own development, and that opportunities for self-development can arise in very ordinary ways at work. Colleagues, for example, often represent a rich vein of knowledge and experience which can be tapped in counselling sessions. He rightly points out that what employees seek out for themselves is likely to make a greater impact than anything received passively from others.

Orlans (1986) argues that counselling is important to help staff in organizations cope with stress and with the problems of overcoming difficulties associated with change. In addition, organizations should set up employee assistance programmes to give individuals the opportunity of participating in counselling interviews. Handy (1989) predicts that in the increasingly flexible, high performance organizations of the future, managers will experience greater pressures than ever before. Kanter (1983, 1989), on the same theme, suggests that there is already evidence that managers work longer hours than ever before. The organizations of the future, she predicts, will bring 'excitement for some, terror for many'. Counselling, therefore, is likely to have an increasingly important part to play in encouraging managers to withstand pressure and progress their development. Counselling is not only a set of techniques associated with non-directive interviewing. It also represents a perspective in recognizing that people are not work machines but individuals with fears, anxieties and problems.

Mentoring

Mentoring refers to the process in which an individual may have regular dialogue with another person – who is usually older and at a more senior level in the organization – on a range of issues relating to the individual's present job, and to career development. The mentoring situation gives the individual an opportunity, in a non-threatening environment, to talk over personal and work issues with a person who should be well placed not only to listen but to offer advice.

The literature suggests (Clutterbuck, 1985; Bragg, 1989) that the mentor should not be the line manager of the individual, to ensure that the mentoring process is not distorted by line management considerations. The line manager has other responsibilities, for example appraising and coaching subordinates, ensuring goals and targets are achieved, influencing promotion decisions. While the line manager has an important role to play with regard to the individual's development through these and other activities, mentoring has a different, though related part to play, in giving the individual access to someone else at a senior level in the organization.

Mentoring, therefore, involves two persons, one senior and one junior, who have regular interaction, including:

- talking over problems, usually relating to the present job, or to career development issues
- listening
- ensuring problems are thoroughly analysed
- identifying and evaluating courses of action for improving job and personal effectiveness
- giving advice
- providing encouragement

- alleviating anxieties
- exploring alternative career paths
- discussing development methods and opportunities.

Kram (1983) had identified two principal forms of mentoring:

- Career-related, where the primary emphasis is on discussing and giving advice on career development issues.
- Psychosocial, where the focus is mainly on helping the individual to understand, and come to terms with, his or her own strengths and weaknesses, to develop a personal identity, and to gain clearer feelings and views of personal competencies.

In most mentoring relationships both elements are likely to be present, although there may be variations in the degree of emphasis placed on the one, relative to the other.

The main benefits of mentoring to an individual are:

- the opportunity to talk through problems and issues with someone at a senior level
- obtaining an alternative view from that of the immediate superior on a range of issues
- facilitating individual development through analysing problems and identifying courses of action that will contribute to the development of the individual
- gaining a clearer personal identity
- greater awareness of career opportunities, and how to achieve them
- greater understanding of how to overcome learning barriers that may be impeding development.

At first sight, it may appear that mentoring will often occur anyway through personal contacts that will exist between junior and senior employees, through the informal organizational networks that develop outside formal line management relationships. Many companies, however, have decided that, to secure the benefits, mentoring must be established in a more systematic fashion. This involves:

- identifying potential mentors
- identifying those individuals who will benefit most from mentoring
- establishing pairings between mentors and individual participants
- setting up a schedule of meetings between mentors and participants
- providing opportunities for mentors and participants to communicate as and when the need arises
- evaluating the process, and the results it has produced.

The benefits of a well-organized mentoring programme accrue not only to the individuals, but also to the mentors themselves, who benefit in terms of:

- having a new objective upon which to focus
- unlocking their experience to help others
- enjoying reflected glory from the achievements of the younger employees they are helping.

In the USA formal mentoring programmes have gained popularity more rapidly than elsewhere. Bragg (1989) estimates that around one-third of large American companies operate mentoring programmes, suggesting that they fall into three broad categories:

1. Formal programmes, usually of twelve-months' duration or longer, that are aimed principally at new recruits with the objective of helping them to settle into the organization and learn the corporate culture rapidly, to assist them to become satisfactory performers at an early stage.
2. Semi-formal programmes where senior managers identify promising young or recently promoted managers, and assist their development through mentoring.
3. Co-worker mentoring, often used by sales forces where, for example, a relatively inexperienced salesperson is paired with a veteran to gain product knowledge and learn selling skills.

Bragg indicates that smaller organizations in the USA are increasingly recognizing the benefits of mentoring, and cites the case of a small software company with eight employees, which gained substantial cost savings by using its internal mentoring programme to teach everyone a new programming language without sending them on expensive external seminars.

There are some risks and challenges inherent in mentoring programmes. Those not included may feel rejected and become demotivated through being omitted. Some may become overdependent on the mentoring relationship.

A major challenge is to ensure that mentoring does not frustrate, but supports the role of the line manager in developing productive working relationships with staff through performance appraisal and the techniques of day-to-day management, including where appropriate the use of coaching and counselling.

References

Allison, T. 1991: Counselling and coaching. In F. Neale (ed.), *Performance Management*. London: IPM.

Beer, M. 1981: Performance appraisal: Dilemmas and possibilities, *Organizational Dynamics*, Winter.

Bragg, A. 1989: *Is a mentor programme in your future? Sales and Marketing Management*, September, 54–63.

Braithwaite, R. and Owen, R. 1989: Developmental career counselling – even high flyers need it. Unpublished paper, presented at IPM Conference, Harrogate, England, October.

Clutterbuck, D. 1985: *Everyone Needs a Mentor*. London: IPM.

Farnsworth, T. 1979. How to develop yourself. *Management Today*, May.

Halson, W. 1990: Teaching supervisors to coach. *Personnel Management*, March.

Handy, C. 1989: *The Age of Unreason*. London: Business Books.

Kanter, R.M. 1983: *The Change Masters*. London: Allen & Unwin.

Kanter, R.M. 1989: *When Giants Learn to Dance*. London: Simon & Schuster.

Knowles, M. 1975: *Self-Directed Learning*. Cambridge: Cambridge Books.

Kram, K.E. 1983: Phases of the mentor relationship. *Academy of Management Journal*, 26 (4).

Mumford, A. 1988: What's new in management development? *Personnel Management*, May.

Neale, F. (ed.) 1991: *The Handbook of Performance Management*. London: IPM.

Novarra, V. 1986: Can a manager be a counsellor? *Personnel Management*, June.

Orlans, V. 1986: Counselling services in organisations. *Personnel Review*, 15 (5).

Peters, T. and Waterman, R. 1982: *In Search of Excellence*. New York: Harper & Row.

Temporal, P. 1982: In M. Woodcock (ed.), *Management Self-Development: Concepts and Practices*. Gower.

12

Monitoring and Reviewing Performance Appraisal

Monitoring and evaluating systems of performance appears to be a substantially neglected area, in theory and in practice. Few of the many management books and articles have much to say on this topic; nor do the majority tend to accord it much importance. Fletcher and Williams (1985) include a chapter on 'Maintenance and evaluation' and suggest that monitoring the progress of a system of performance appraisal is vital to its effectiveness. Yet many companies which operate systems of performance appraisal appear to have given little thought and effort to monitoring how well their systems are operating, even with systems that have been in operation for many years.

The Importance of Monitoring and Reviewing the Performance Appraisal System

Monitoring and evaluation have short-term and long-term dimensions. The term 'monitoring' will be used to refer to the short-term requirement to ensure that the various elements of the cycle take place in the way intended, and according to timescales developed in setting objectives and developing a plan for the performance appraisal cycle. This responsibility for monitoring the system of performance appraisal is usually undertaken by the personnel, training or human resource function in medium-sized and large organizations. In smaller organizations without personnel and training specialists, there is a need to ensure one individual has responsibility for monitoring the performance appraisal system. The ideal person for this task is often the 'champion' of the performance appraisal system. Such a person will normally be committed to the concept, and to the organization's plans for implementation. The dangers in any organization are that the person to whom the monitoring responsibility is entrusted:

- is at too junior level to influence senior managers
- has many other duties, and devotes little time and/or low priority to this task
- has not had sufficient prior involvement with the appraisal scheme to understand fully all its characteristics
- is not sufficiently well known in the organization, so that appraisers and appraisees may be less inclined to approach them with queries which, if not resolved, could effect the successful implementation of the system of performance appraisal.

If any or all of these factors are present, it is unlikely that the performance appraisal system will be fully and effectively implemented. Likely symptoms of trouble will include patchy implementation – some parts of the organization enthusiastic, other parts less so; non-completion or slow completion of appraisal documents; and ambiguity over roles of line managers and personnel and training specialists, in terms of ensuring follow-up actions, agreed at appraisal interviews, actually take place.

The last aspect is a particularly important area where energetic monitoring is required. Research studies (for example, Anderson and Barnett, 1986) show that even in well-organized and well-run appraisal systems only a proportion of actions planned and agreed by appraisers and appraisees subsequently are implemented. Anderson and Barnett (1987) highlight that the organization culture and the extent to which appraisers and appraisees have positive attitudes towards appraisal processes will impact on the probability of useful follow-up actions, agreed at the appraisal interview, taking place.

Many writers (e.g. Brinkerhoff and Kanter, 1980) have drawn attention to the fact that the credibility and sustainability of performance appraisal systems depends to a large extent on actions agreed at appraisal interviews being implemented. Monitoring is particularly crucial in this area. Part of the monitoring function may involve clarifying the interface between line managers on the one hand, and personnel and training specialists on the other. It is all too easy for non-action to result through expecting some other party to take charge of follow-up action.

Reviewing is assumed here to refer to the longer-term process of evaluating the system after the completion of one or more performance appraisal cycles. The purpose of reviewing is to assess the extent to which the objectives of the system are being achieved, and the plan for implementation is taking place.

Reviewing can take several forms, for example:

- Statistical analysis of ratings to check for bias and leniency effects, to permit comparisons between departments and divisions, and develop overall company distributions.
- Questionnaire surveys to gather factual data (for example, on periods of notice given for appraisal interviews, and lengths of interviews) and attitudinal data, on the perceptions and views of key parties towards appraisal.
- Individual and group interviews.

A plan for a study to review the effectiveness of the system of performance appraisal in the UK operation of a large US multinational corporation is shown in appendix 12.1. As can be seen, the study involves interviews with key parties and a questionnaire that can be distributed to a large sample of appraisers and appraisees in the organization. You can see from the questionnaire that while the precise set of questions should be formulated to generate data relevant to the organization's needs, some common elements are likely to be present:

An initial section which gathers data about the characteristics of the respondents – for example age, sex, educational level, length of time in the organization and in the present job, job function, job level. This data permits various forms of analysis to be carried out; for instance, whether any of these factors are important in explaining differences in appraisal practices, or in attitudes towards performance appraisal.

One or more sections that gather attitudinal data about performance appraisal. As can be seen in part 2 of the questionnaire, such data is collected through a set of five-point rating scales that measure the direction and strength of views on various appraisal issues. This type of approach facilitates the analysis of results by computer.

One or more sections examining appraisal practices, and attitudes towards performance appraisal from the appraisee perspective (see part 3).

Clearly timing can be important; if too much time has elapsed since the most recent appraisal interview, appraisees may have difficulty in recalling what happened very precisely.

One or more sections examining appraisal practices, and attitudes towards performance appraisal from the appraiser perspective (see part 5).

This approach permits the analysis of differences in perception between appraisers and appraisees regarding the same appraisal interviews. Several studies (Anderson and Watt, 1988; Lawler, Mohrman and Resnick-West, 1984) highlight important differences of perception, with implications for the effective training of both sets of parties.

The investigation of background information relevant to performance appraisal (see part 4). This could include the investigation of the extent to which appraisers and appraisees communicate on a regular, informal basis, a factor that some studies (Fletcher, 1978) have shown to be significant in explaining how performance appraisal is likely to be perceived.

While multiple-choice questions aid computer analysis of the results, and make easier the interpretation of results, it is desirable to include at least one open-ended question – probably at the end of the questionnaire – to permit respondents to express views on appraisal issues not covered in any of the multiple-choice questions. Sample sizes should be kept as large as is realistically possible to ensure that information of a representative nature is being obtained, especially since follow-up analysis involving, say, particular age groups or particular functions can quickly lead to much smaller numbers of respondents being examined.

Since many employees view performance appraisal as a sensitive area, and may be concerned about the protection of anonymity in expressing their views, some external party who is seen as unbiased, is often employed to conduct this type of questionnaire survey.

As indicated in appendix 12.1, the questionnaire survey can be supported by a number of interviews – in this example, with a sample drawn from senior management, appraisers and appraisees. The aims of these interviews are:

1. To clarify senior management thinking, and expectations relating to the system of performance appraisal.
2. To investigate in depth issues that emerge from the analysis of questionnaires.

Normally, semi-structured or structured interviews are used. A structured interview implies the preparation in advance of a set of questions put to all those who belong to a particular group of those selected for interview. In the example shown, four variants of the schedule of questions to be used in conducting interviews would have to be prepared – for the senior management, appraiser, appraisee groups and for the Head of Personnel. The outline question schedules for the interviews with senior managers and with the Head of Personnel are shown in appendix 12.1. In particular organizational contexts, depending on the nature and coverage of the system of performance appraisal, other groups – for example, trade union representatives – may be included in the interview programme.

Another option is to consider using structured interviews as a replacement for, instead of in addition to, the questionnaire survey, especially if there are serious concerns about the percentage of respondents who are likely to complete and return questionnaires. Around a 50 per cent response rate, as a generality, is likely to be acceptable, especially if the sample to whom the questionnaire is distributed is large. The response rate can be much better. Anderson and Barnett (1986) report an 88 per cent rate in a questionnaire survey distributed to members of the nursing profession in the Scottish Health Authority of Fife.

When interviews support a questionnaire survey, semi-structured interviews are likely to be used, where interviewers may deviate from the prepared schedule of questions to probe particular issues or responses.

The data generated from a questionnaire survey, in some cases amplified by data from an interview programme, can be used for several purposes:

- To assess how effectively the system is operating.
- To find out attitudes towards performance appraisal, and the particular system being implemented.
- To clarify and define problems and issues relating to the design and implementation of the system.
- To provide feedback to appraisers and appraisees – the data can provide a basis for the formulation of refresher training programmes.
- To evaluate performance appraisal training.

Where real benefits are seen to emerge, organizational policy may lead to a review exercise as described in this chapter being carried out, not as a 'one-off' exercise, but on a periodic basis, say every two, three or four years.

References

Anderson, G.C. and Barnett, J.G. 1986: Nurse appraisal in practice. *The Health Service Journal*, October.

Anderson, G.C. and Barnett, J.G. 1987: The characteristics of effective appraisal interviews. *Personnel Review*, 16 (4).

Anderson, G.C. and Watt, E. 1988: A new context for performance appraisal. *Health Care Management*, 3 (1).

Brinkerhoff, D.W. and Kanter, R.M. 1980: Appraising the performance of performance appraisal. *Sloan Management Review*, Spring.

Fletcher, C.A. 1978: Manager subordinate communication and leadership Style: A field study of their relationship to perceived outcomes of appraisal interviews. *Personnel Review*, 7 (1).

Fletcher, C.A. and Williams, R. 1985: *Performance Appraisal and Career Development*. London: Hutchinson.

Lawler, E.E., Mohrman, A.M. and Resnick-West, S.M. 1984: Performance appraisal revisited. *Organizational Dynamics*, Summer.

Appendix 12.1

Research Project into Performance Appraisal

Aims

To study how effectively the performance appraisal scheme is operating, by examining the views and attitudes of various parties – top management and a sample of appraisers and appraisees – regarding:

- General beliefs about performance appraisal.
- The objectives of performance appraisal.
- Identifying and measuring what happened in performance appraisal interviews.
- Identifying and measuring the outcomes of appraisal interviews.
- Identifying and measuring some of the determinants of appraisal interviewing effectiveness.
- Assessing the effectiveness of the performance appraisal training programme.

In addition, it is hoped that recommendations will emerge for the further development and refinement of the appraisal scheme to achieve both corporate and individual objectives.

Methods

Questionnaire survey.
Interviews with a small number of senior managers, the Head of Personnel, with a sample of appraisers and appraisees.

Report

The report produced and feedback on its findings will be given to the company.

Performance appraisal questionnaire

We are conducting a survey on performance appraisal. The aim is to give you an opportunity to express your views on performance appraisal in [company name].

Part 1 relates to you and your position in the company.
Part 2 examines general attitudes towards performance appraisal.
Part 3 relates to your experience at your most recent appraisal interview conducted by your boss.
Part 4 investigates background information relevant to performance appraisal.
Part 5 should only be completed if you carry out appraisal interviews for staff who report to you.
Part 6 should only be completed if you attended one of the $1\frac{1}{2}$ day performance appraisal training programmes organized by the company.

CONFIDENTIALITY All views expressed in the questionnaire will be treated with maximum confidentiality. In particular, no information will be released which would permit the views of any individual to be identified.

Performance appraisal questionnaire

Part 1   Information about you

Please read each question carefully and answer by ringing the number *opposite* the appropriate answer, unless otherwise stated.

		For office use only
1. Please state your job grade:	———	
2. Please indicate the area in which you work:		
F. production	1	
F. engineering/QA	2	
C. production	3	
C. engineering/QA	4	
Personnel	5	
Finance/Purchasing	6	
DP/DC	7	
Manufacturing services (including industrial and plant engineering)	8	
Other . . . please state	9	

3. How many subordinates report directly to you? _____
4. For how many of your subordinates have you
   conducted appraisals?

5. Please indicate your age group:	Under 26	1
	26–35	2
	36–45	3
	Over 45	4
6. How long have you been in your present job?	Less than 6 months	1
	6 months to 1 year	2
	1 year to 3 years	3
	3 years to 5 years	4
	5 years or more	5
7. How long have you been in the Company:	Less than 6 months	1
	6 months to 1 year	2
	1 year to 3 years	3
	3 years to 5 years	4
	5 years or more	5
8. Have you had first-hand experience of performance appraisal with any previous employer?	Yes	1
	No	1
9. How many appraisal interviews have you had in this company?	0	1
	1 or 2	2
	3 or more	3
10. How many appraisal interviews have you had with your present boss?	0	1
	1 or 2	2
	3 or more	3

Part 2   *General attitudes towards performance appraisal*

1. Performance appraisal helps to develop a better understanding between superiors and subordinates.	Strongly agree	1
	Agree	2
	Neutral	3
	Disagree	4
	Strongly disagree	5
2. Performance appraisal makes a useful contribution to the Company by encouraging people to perform more productively in their jobs.	Strongly agree	1
	Agree	2
	Neutral	3
	Disagree	4
	Strongly disagree	5

3. A subordinate's self-appraisal   Strongly agree   1
   should be an important part   Agree   2
   of performance appraisal.   Neutral   3
      Disagree   4
      Strongly disagree   5

4. Salary discussions should be   Strongly agree   1
   based on the ratings and   Agree   2
   contents of performance   Neutral   3
   appraisal reports.   Disagree   4
      Strongly disagree   5

5. Promotion decisions should   Strongly agree   1
   be based on the ratings and   Agree   2
   contents of performance   Neutral   3
   appraisal reports.   Disagree   4
      Strongly disagree   5

6. Performance Appraisal   Strongly agree   1
   should be based largely on   Agree   2
   the immediate boss's ratings   Neutral   3
   of employee performance.   Disagree   4
      Strongly disagree   5

7. Performance appraisal   Strongly agree   1
   should also involve the   Agree   2
   views of several managers   Neutral   3
   who can comment from   Disagree   4
   first-hand knowledge on   Strongly disagree   5
   the employee's performance.

8. As regards   I am strongly in favour of it   1
   performance   I am slightly in favour of it   2
   appraisal in   I am neither for nor against it   3
   general: I am slightly against it   4
      I am strongly against it   5

Part 3 Your most recent appraisal interview

This section relates to your most recent appraisal
interview with your boss.

1. How much notice   1 day or less   1
   were you given?   2–3 days   2
      4–7 days   3
      More than 1 week   4

2. How long did your appraisal interview last?	Under 25 minutes	1
	25–40 minutes	2
	40 minutes–1 hour	3
	Over 1 hour	4
3. Which of the following was *most* time spent in discussing?	Your strengths	1
	Your weaknesses	2
	Ways of improving your performance	3
4. Which of the following was *least* time spent in discussing?	Your strengths	1
	Your weaknesses	2
	Ways of improving your performance	3
5. At the interview did you find your boss's attitude:	Highly supportive	1
	Slightly supportive	2
	Neutral	3
	Slightly negative	4
	Highly negative	5
6. Did you undertake any preparations for your appraisal interview	Yes	1
	No	2

If Yes, please answer Question 7; if No, please proceed to Question 8.

7. If you did undertake preparations, please indicate how much time approximately you spent preparing for the interview.	Less than half an hour	1
	Half an hour to one hour	2
	1 hour to 2 hours	3
	Over 2 hours	4
8. To what extent did you feel threatened in the appraisal interview?	To a substantial extent	1
	To some extent	2
	To a limited extent	3
	Not at all	4

9. Did the interview discussion centre:
Primarily on your job performance?   1
On both your job performance, and on your
   personality, but with more emphasis on your
   job performance?   2

For office
use only

On both your job performance, and on your
personality, but with more emphasis on your
personality?   3
Primarily on your personality?   4
On other matters?   5
  Please specify

_____

_____

10. Did completion of the self-assessment sections help the discussion at your appraisal interview?	Not at all	1
	To a slight extent	2
	To some extent	3
	To a substantial extent	4
11. Were you able to put forward and discuss your ideas and feelings at the interview?	Hardly at all	1
	To a modest extent	2
	To a reasonable extet	3
	To a substantial extent	4
12. Please estimate, approximately, the the percentages of time you contributed to the discussion at the interview.	Over 70%	1
	50–70%	2
	30–50%	3
	Less than 30%	4
13. At the end of the interview did you feel:	Encouraged	1
	Neutral/slightly encouraged	2
	Neutral/slightly discouraged	3
	Discouraged	4
14. Did you feel your boss's assessment of your performance was:	Extremely fair	1
	Reasonably fair	2
	Not too fair	3
	Very unfair	4
15. Has your performance improved as a result of your interview?	Hardly at all	1
	To a slight extent	2
	To some extent	3
	To a substantial extent	4
	I don't know	5

16. How much   No importance   1
    importance did   Modest in importance   2
    you attach to   Reasonable importance   3
    the interview?   Substantial importance   4

17. Has the interview had any impact on relations
    between you and your boss?
    Relationships now much more positive   1
    Relationships largely unchanged/slightly more
        positive   2
    Relationships largely unchanged/slightly more
        negative   3
    Relationships now much more negative   4
    No longer work for the person who conducted
        my last interview   5

18. Was there   Yes, to a substantial extent 1
    adequate   Yes, to some extent   2
    opportunity to   Not really, very limited   3
    discuss your future None   4
    in the Company?

19. Did you receive   Yes, to a substantial extent 1
    accurate and useful Yes, to some extent   2
    feedback on how   Not really, very limited   3
    your boss feels you None   4
    are getting on in
    your job?

20. To what extent   To a substantial extent   1
    did you and your To some extent   2
    boss agree in   To a limited extent   3
    setting future   Not at all   4
    objectives and
    targets in your work?

21. Were follow-up   To a substantial extent   1
    actions agreed to To some extent   2
    improve your   To a limited extent   3
    performance?   Not at all   4

22. Were your training To a substantial extent   1
    and development   To some extent   2
    requirements   To a limited extent   3
    accurately defined? Not at all   4

For office
use only

23. Indicate which of the following were planned at your interview to assist your development (please circle as many categories as are applicable) and whether they subsequently occurred.

Attendance at external course. Planned?	Yes	1
	No	2
Subsequently occurred?	Yes	1
	No	2
Attendance at internal course. Planned?	Yes	1
	No	2
Subsequently occurred?	Yes	1
	No	2
Coaching (guidance on the job). Planned?	Yes	1
	No	2
Subsequently occurred?	Yes	1
	No	2
Self-development activities. Planned?	Yes	1
	No	2
Subsequently occurred?	Yes	1
	No	2
Special projects. Planned?	Yes	1
	No	2
Subsequently occurred?	Yes	1
	No	2

Others (please specify)

_____

_____

Part 4   Background information

This section covers background information relevant to performance appraisal.

1. How often do you and your boss discuss your work performance apart from in the appraisal interview?	Frequently	1
	Sometimes	2
	Rarely	3
	Never	4

For office
use only

2. Please indicate the category which most closely describes the managerial style of your boss.

Makes decisions on his or her own usually, without seeking views of staff	1
Makes decisions on his or her own usually, after consulting with staff	2
Likes to involve staff in the making of decisions	3
None of these	4

3. Is the approach adopted by your boss in the appraisal interview similar or different from his or her normal managerial style?

Very similar	1
Fairly similar	2
Slightly different	3
Very different	4

4. Please indicate the style of manager you prefer working for.

Autocratic	1
Consultative	2
Democratic	3

5. Please indicate how frequently your boss coaches you (i.e. provides you with on-the-job guidance and instruction) to help you develop your performance.

Very frequently (more than once per week)	1
Fairly often (once or twice a fortnight)	2
Occasionally	3
Never	4

6. How adequate do you find the coaching provided by your boss?

Very adequate	1
Reasonably adequate	2
Barely adequate	3
Inadequate	4

Part 5 Interviewers

This section should only be completed by those who conduct appraisal interviews for staff who report to them.

1. Please indicate number of staff for whom you conduct appraisal interviews:

For office
use only

2. How much time do
you normally spend
preparing for a
typical appraisal
interview with a
member of your staff?

Less than half hour	1
Half hour–1 hour	2
1–2 hours	3
Over 2 hours	4

3. How long, on average,
are the appraisal
interviews you
conduct with members
of your staff?

Under 25 minutes	1
25–40 minutes	2
40 minutes–1 hour	3
Over 1 hour	4

4. On average, for what
percentage of the time
does the appraisee
contribute to the
discussion?

Over 70%	1
50–70%	2
30–50%	3
Less than 30%	4

5. In your view, to what
extent, on average,
do appraisees feel
threatened in
appraisal interviews?

To a substantial extent	1
To some extent	2
To a limited extent	3
Not at all	4

6. Do appraisal
interviews have any
impact on relations
between you and
your staff?

Relationships much more positive	1
Relationships largely unchanged/slightly more positive	2
Relationships largely unchanged/slightly more negative	3
Relationships much more negative	4

7. At the end
of appraisal
interviews with
your staff do you
feel, on average:

Encouraged	1
Neutral/slightly encouraged	2
Neutral/slightly discouraged	3
Discouraged	4

8. Do you encounter
any major difficulties
in planning for, or
conducting appraisal
interviews?

Yes	1
No	2

9. If Yes, please give brief details

_____

_____

10. Are there any problems which in your view prevents
the performance appraisal scheme being implemented
as effectively as should be the case?
Please record

_____

_____

_____

11. In general, what results do you feel accrue from
the performance appraisal scheme?
Please record

_____

_____

_____

Part 6   Performance appraisal training programme

This section should be completed by those who attended
the $1\frac{1}{2}$ day performance appraisal training programme.

1. How useful was the   Of substantial value   1
performance   Of some value   2
appraisal training   Of limited value   3
programme in   Of no value   4
increasing your
understanding of
performance appraisal?

2. How useful was   Of substantial value   1
the performance   Of some value   2
appraisal training   Of limited value   3
programme in   Of no value   4
briefing you on the
new performance
appraisal scheme?

For office
use only

3. How useful was   Of substantial value   1
   the performance   Of some value   2
   appraisal training   Of limited value   3
   programme in   Of no value   4
   developing your
   appraisal interviewing
   skills?
4. How useful did   Of substantial value   1
   you find role-   Of some value   2
   playing as a training   Of limited value   3
   method in developing   Of no value   4
   interviewing skills?
5. What further training, if any, would help you to
   conduct appraisal interviews more confidently and
   effectively?
   (Please circle as many categories as appropriate.)
   Appreciation of the objectives of the performance
   appraisal scheme and how it operates   1
   Completion of forms   2
   Interviewing techniques   3
   Coaching skills   4
6. How often do you   Every year   1
   feel refresher   Every 2 or 3 years   2
   training in   At 4-year intervals, or more 3
   performance   Not at all   4
   appraisal and
   appraisal interviewing
   should be provided?

THE END

Thank you for your co-operation in completing this
questionnaire. Completed questionnaires should be returned
to [name].

Interview: Senior managers

Aims

Find out senior management views on organizational role of performance appraisal, and level of involvement/commitment of senior management.

Specific questions

What do you see as the objectives of performance appraisal?
What do you consider are the priorities among objectives?
Why did the organization introduce it in the first place?
What, in your view, have been its main achievements?
What are your views on separation of evaluation of performance/ potential/rewards?
How is performance of top management evaluated?
Role of appraiser: Personal experiences:
Role of reviewer: Personal experiences:
Role of appraisee: Personal experiences:
What is your experience of performance appraisal in other organizations?
What has been the influence of this experience?
What are the ways in which you would like to see performance appraisal developed?
What is the amount of time devoted by top management to:
(a) evaluating performance and potential;
(b) discussing issues relating to the appraisal scheme.
What are your views on monitoring performance appraisal?
What are your views on conditions required for successful appraisal?
What are your views on:
(a) Self-appraisal?
(b) Multi-appraisal?
(c) Peer or team appraisal?
(d) Openness?
(e) Handling change in performance appraisal?
(f) Research questions in performance appraisal that should be investigated?
(g) Problems associated with performance appraisal?

Interview: Head of Personnel

Aims

To gather data about: background to appraisal scheme; appraisal objectives; appraisal design; systems; procedures.

Special questions

Why was formal appraisal introduced?
What are the appraisal objectives?
Prioitize your objectives.
Achievement of appraisal – which objectives have best been achieved?
Weaknesses/limitations?
Plans for overcoming these?
Separate reviews for appraising current performance/potential/rewards?
Policy on openness?
Resolving conflict in appraisals?
Signing-off procedures?
Retention of appraisal documents?
Use analysis of appraisal data?
Monitoring follow-up action.
Policy on training appraisers/appraisees?
Methods of rating potential?
Links between appraisal and succession planning?
Role of personnel and training re performance appraisal?
What are your personal views on:
(a) Self-appraisal?
(b) Multi-appraisal?
(c) Openness?
(d) Conditions required for effective appraisal?
(e) Handling change in performance appraisal?
Policies on coaching/counselling/monitoring/communications

13

Case Studies
A. Scottish Nuclear Ltd

Scottish Nuclear Ltd is a relatively new company, established in March 1990, having formerly been part of the South of Scotland Electricity Board (SSEB). The organizational changes, which led to the creation of Scottish Power, in place of the SSEB and the emergence of Scottish Nuclear resulted from government-initiated changes concerned with privatizing the electricity industry.

In December 1989 Scottish Nuclear received a performance appraisal scheme from Scottish Power, a scheme which had been developed in the final period of the existence of the SSEB. The new scheme was introduced in mid-1990, for senior managers only. Scottish Nuclear's senior personnel and training staff recognized some problems both with the scheme itself, and with the fact that the scheme had been designed for a different organization.

Several options were considered:

1. Abandon the scheme, and develop a new system of performance appraisal from scratch.
2. Introduce the SSEB/Scottish Power system.
3. Use the scheme as a foundation for tailoring a system of performance appraisal to meet the requirements of Scottish Nuclear.

Not surprisingly, the decision was taken towards the end of 1990 to follow option 3. Over the next fifteen months, in collaboration with the author of this book as consultant, a number of changes were introduced.

Problem Identification

The first step was to identify the deficiencies associated with the scheme which had been introduced, given that it had not been received with enthusiasm by most of the senior managers who were the initial group to be covered by it. The senior personnel and training staff were concerned that unless the scheme was designed and implemented in an effective way, to the satisfaction of senior managers, then it would be difficult to build upon what the senior personnel and training staff saw as shaky foundations for extending the scheme to other groups of employees. The main problems identified were:

The imposed nature of the scheme. Little or no consultation had taken place with managers or employees during the design phase. A large company of external consultants had been commissioned to design the system. Accordingly, the senior managers of Scottish Nuclear did not have feelings of ownership towards the scheme.

Exclusive emphasis on objectives. Much careful thought had obviously been devoted to the scheme with the emphasis, in keeping with modern thinking on performance appraisal, on setting objectives and subsequently evaluating performance against objectives. It was felt, however, that the exclusive use of objectives without any other criteria for evaluating performance was a deficiency. Process measures were considered important for inclusion, to give a better, all-round picture of performance, since someone could be achieving objectives but at a cost, in terms of, for example, upsetting other groups of people inside and outside the organization. Accordingly it was decided that a set of core skills would be introduced, to examine some of the personal competencies of managers and aspects of behaviour to focus on their methods of managing, as well as on their achievement of objectives.

Relationship of performance appraisal objectives to central job purpose. It appeared that in its original formulation the performance appraisal scheme encouraged appraisers to set objectives for their staff that were largely associated with new and innovative aspects of jobs. The view was expressed that this was wrong, and that objectives agreed through the performance appraisal system should reflect the central purpose of managers' jobs. Objectives for members of staff could therefore be set in areas of regular, continuing activity, as well as in new areas of activity.

The Design Process

The senior personnel and training staff decided to hold several one-day seminars for senior managers, designed to help them to develop both their understanding of performance appraisal and their appraisal skills, and to provide a medium for consultation with them on how the system of performance appraisal could be modified and improved to meet more closely their needs, and the needs of their staffs. These seminars led to:

1. General support from the senior management group both for the concept of performance appraisal and for the company's planned system, modified in several ways. The senior managers generally welcomed the idea of a more broadly based system that included the assessment of core skills as well as the evaluation of performance against objectives.
2. Recognition of the value of introducing a six-month review when, without excessive paperwork, a formal check could be made on progress towards objectives which would normally be evaluated on a twelve-month basis. The mid-year review would also provide, if appropriate, a useful opportunity to revise objectives or reassign priorities, in the light of changing business circumstances. Originally it was envisaged that a mid-year review would be initiated only by appraisees, not appraisers.
3. A view, expressed by the majority of senior managers, that the coverage of performance appraisal should be extended within the organization to include middle and junior levels of management.

The Objectives, Methods, and Cycle of Activities of the Scottish Nuclear System of Performance Appraisal

Objectives

The main purposes of the performance appraisal system are:

1.   To provide an opportunity for discussion of a job-holder's performance during the previous twelve months based around the attainment of agreed individual objectives but also including an assessment of certain core skills essential to satisfactory performance. This discussion will take place between the two people best able to assess this: the job-holder and his or her immediate manager.
2.   To identify the job-holder's scope for development within his or her job, by setting individual objectives for the next twelve months that are realistic, meaningful and measurable, as well as challenging.
3.   To identify training and development needs that will enable the job-holder to do the job better, thus making an increased contribution to meeting the objectives of the company as a whole.

Methods and the performance appraisal cycle

The core of the scheme is seen to be the appraisal interview, held annually between the job-holder and the immediate manager, called the reporting officer. The results of the appraisal interview are recorded on the staff performance appraisal form.

The performance appraisal cycle takes place over a twelve-month period, and begins and ends with the appraisal interview. In the performance appraisal interview, the reporting officer is expected to hold an open discussion with the job-holder covering:

- Performance over the previous twelve months.
- Core skills.
- The setting of objectives for the next twelve months.
- Training and development needs.

After the appraisal interview, the completed appraisal document is returned to the local personnel departments. There are three personnel locations – at headquarters in Glasgow, and at the two power stations, Torness and Hunterston. The appraisal form requires a six-point rating scale to be completed for each of the core-skills, and a five-point overall rating scale. The thinking is that the whole should not be a simple addition of the component parts. The attainment of objectives as well as the assessment of core skills contributes to the overall rating.

The other elements of the performance appraisal cycle are shown in appendix 13.1. It is envisaged that about six to eight weeks after the appraisal interview, a review of future potential will be carried out. The reviewing officer (normally the appraiser or reporting officer's line manager who reviews and countersigns appraisal reports) completes a future potential form during a meeting with the reporting officer and a representative of the Personnel Department. The content of the document completed covers the areas of the appraisee's immediate and long-term career potential. The appraisee is not present at the meeting.

Acting on the information generated is seen as a prime responsibility for line managers, in that they are expected to encourage and develop the staff who report to them within their current jobs and for future career opportunities where appropriate. The role of the personnel function is to give support to line managers through providing services such as training courses, management development and manpower planning systems.

The six-monthly review is a meeting which enables the reporting officer to review with the appraisee objectives set and agreed at the appraisal interview six months before. A reminder about the six-monthly review is provided to both the appraiser and appraisee.

At a suitable time before the twelve-months period has elapsed, the Personnel Department will issue the paperwork needed for the next appraisal interview.

Objective setting

As already noted, setting objectives is a central, though not the only element of performance appraisal in the company.

The approach is that six objectives should be set for each jobholder, related to aspects of the corporate objectives. Two of the six – efficiency improvement and quality improvement – are fixed for all staff. The other four can be flexibly selected, either as additional objectives concerned with efficiency improvement and quality improvement or from the areas of: business development; safety; staff management; personnel development; communication; problem-solving.

In setting objectives, the company provides the following guidelines:

- They must be directly relevant to the work carried out by the appraisee.
- The range of objectives should reflect the breadth of the appraisee's job, and not just part of it.
- They must be 'influenceable' by the appraisee through his or her own efforts in carrying out the job.

Appraisers are asked to establish a priority among the objectives agreed with each appraisee, and this priority will be reflected in the order in which they are listed on the appraisal document.

Performance management

The company advocates a performance management philosophy in encouraging both appraisers and appraisees to think of objective-setting not as a 'once-off' event but as a process which requires monitoring, guidance, discussion and feedback on a regular basis, to increase the probability of objectives being achieved.

Core skills

These are defined as those competencies that are fundamental to an employee's performance and the way in which he or she carries out job tasks. While the assessment of objectives is important in assessing performance over the previous twelve months, core skills are those which contribute to long-term success and development.

A 'long list' of core skills was initially developed, and these were reduced largely through a process of consultation involving senior managers and senior personnel and training staff to eight key categories, shown in appendix 13.2. For each of the eight areas of core skills a brief description is provided, to clarify the standard expected of job holders. Each core skill is assessed on a six-point rating scale, with provision for explanatory comments. Comment is particularly encouraged where there is significant over or under performance in a particular category, where a particular core skill is of little significance to the job-holder (or alternatively where it is a key element), or where the level of performance represents a development need.

Outcomes from the Performance Appraisal Process

Scottish Nuclear recognizes that a substantial amount of information will emerge from its system of performance appraisal. The company has committed itself to making the best use of this information to its own benefit, and to the benefit of its staff.

The specific outcomes are seen as follows:

1. The setting of work-related objectives so that staff have a clear picture of what is expected of them, and how their work contributes to corporate objectives.
2. The review of objectives on a continuous basis so that both managers and staff can work together towards achieving higher levels of performance.
3. The measurement of objectives, to give an accurate picture of what has been achieved, and identify areas where development is needed.
4. Identification of training and development needs, to be used to draw up appropriate off-the-job and on-the-job training programmes as well as transfers and secondments. A positive commitment has been given by the company to act on the information generated, to bring out the best in staff and develop them within their present jobs.

5. Manpower and succession planning, to provide planned career development for staff and to ensure that adequate trained and experienced people are available to fill key posts in the company.
6. Scottish Nuclear views its system of performance appraisal as an important element of its plan to create a positive, forward-looking culture within which individuals will be given considerable freedom within clear parameters to perform.

Progress to Date

The implementation has progressed reasonably well, although two early problems have been identified:

1. Lack of precise formulation of objectives emerging from some appraisal interviews.
2. Tendency to lenient ratings.

Training programmes, and some redefinition and redesign of ratings have so far been used as remedies.

Training Programmes

To date the company has placed considerable emphasis on providing training and briefing for appraisers and appraisees, very much in keeping with best practice recommended in the literature.

Future Issues

Major issues now facing Scottish Nuclear with regard to its system of performance appraisal are:

1. How to create a soundly based link between performance appraisal and individual merit pay awards for senior managers.
2. How far it should cascade the performance appraisal system down the organization to include larger numbers of staff. It is recognized that a new variant may have to be designed for the scheme if lower level employees are to be included. At present, the prevailing view, probably justified, is that expansion of numbers of employees to be covered by the scheme should take place only when the soundness of the scheme as it presently exists has been properly tested and evaluated.

Subsequent Developments

Following the arrival of a new chief executive in the early months of 1992, greater emphasis has been placed on ensuring that objectives that are related to the overall business objectives of the company are being clearly set for senior managers, and external consultants were engaged to assist this process. In addition, top management took the view that the appraisal documentation should be simplified, and a new shortened four-page appraisal form has been prepared (see appendix 13.2). The system of performance appraisal is still being developed. So far future potential reviews have not been held, and this aspect of the system is still under review.

B. Fife Education Authority

The Scottish Office Education Department issued national guidelines in January 1991 for the introduction of staff development and appraisal schemes for teachers in Scottish schools. The impetus for this development came from a desire to find better ways to manage staff development. Staff development was defined as 'the full range of planned activities and experiences which contribute to maintaining and developing professional expertise'. Greater emphasis on staff development was seen as important in ensuring the quality of learning and teaching in schools, as well as assisting the development of teachers' skills in a changing educational world. Pilot studies carried out in 1988/89 demonstrated the central contribution of the appraisal of individual teacher performance to the process of staff development.

The national guidelines are intended to provide a sound basis upon which Scotland's twelve educational authorities can develop staff development and appraisal schemes to suit their local circumstances. The authorities were asked to submit plans for their schemes to the Secretary of State for approval by a specified date in 1990.

The national guidelines identified four groups of purposes for a formal system of performance appraisal operating within an overall context of staff management and development:

1. *Motivation and communication* – providing a formal mechanism for two-way discussion between teachers and their appraisers; enhancing the motivation of teachers by giving them a better understanding of school policies and an opportunity to comment on their implementation and development.
2. *Review, evaluation and development of professional performance* – a periodic, formal opportunity for teachers to receive recognition for achievements, and to discuss with their appraisers how to face up to, and overcome problems and issues affecting their performance.

3. *Identification of personal staff development needs* – in a one-to-one situation with appraisers, discussions take place to identify the personal development needs of teachers, and how these can be met.
4. *Career review* – a regular and systematic procedure to review career development issues, and for appraisers to offer advice and support.

Principles for the Management of Appraisal

A number of general principles for the management of performance appraisal, intended to assist education authorities in developing their schemes, were laid down in the national guidelines. These included:

A. All appraisers and appraisees to receive training before they become involved in the appraisal process.
B. Appraisers should normally be immediate line managers.
C. In the case of headteachers, the appraiser will be a member of, or a representative of the directorate as line manager, assisted by another headteacher.
D. Appraisals to be based on job descriptions relating to the full responsibilities of appraisees, and including individual objectives and targets – job descriptions to be determined by appraisers in consultation with appraisees.
E. The acquisition of first-hand knowledge of classroom practice of the appraisee (where this appears in the individual's job description – clearly the case for most class teachers but not necessarily for headteachers or their deputies) should form a part of the information-gathering process of the appraiser.

The Fife Staff Development and Appraisal Scheme

Fife is one of Scotland's twelve education authorities. The Fife scheme sets the appraisal process firmly within a context of professional development, viewing performance appraisal as part of a wider continuum of professional development which takes place within the existing planning and reviewing work of schools.

The intention was to implement the Staff Development and Appraisal Scheme starting with headteachers in 1991/92 and ensuring that all class teachers will have been appraised at least once by 1995/96. The thinking is that the appraisal system should begin with the assessment of headteachers to ensure that institutional plans and needs are established early in the process. In Fife, in accordance with the national guidelines, the appraisal of headteachers follows broadly the same process as for other teachers, except that a third person is involved. The appraiser for headteachers is a member of the Directorate assisted by a 'visiting' headteacher, who is a headteacher colleague with appropriate experience and skills nominated by the Director of Education to undertake this role. As the scheme is extended, it is envisaged that all headteachers will be given the opportunity to take part in the appraisal scheme as a visiting headteacher.

The process and timings for the appraisal of a headteacher is shown in appendix 13.3, and for class teachers in appendix 13.4. In the case of class teachers, as well as holders of promoted posts such as principal teachers and assistant heads, the appraiser will normally be the immediate line manager.

Features of the Fife scheme

Features that give distinctiveness to the Fife scheme include:

Emphasis on classroom observation While encouraged in the national guidelines, the Fife scheme places great emphasis on classroom observation, making it an essential part of the appraisal process. It is felt this element is not only important for the effective development of staff to take place, but also to help the external credibility of the scheme by showing that systematic information-gathering and evaluation, on a first-hand basis, takes place in the most central area of a teacher's activities.

Focus on self-assessment In the case of all teachers, self-review is seen as a key element in the process, to encourage individuals to reflect carefully and systematically on their professional achievement and on their professional training and development needs. A copy of the questions in the self-review document which individuals are asked to complete is shown in appendix 13.5.

Inclusion of a debriefing meeting This is a unique feature of the Fife scheme – the inclusion of a debriefing meeting, after the appraisal interview has been completed, when both appraiser and appraisees meet to reflect on the whole appraisal process. These debriefing meetings are intended to keep the system dynamic, by encouraging appraisers and appraisees to refine their approaches by learning from their experiences.

The appraisal of headteachers

The approach adopted is an interesting mix of line manager and peer appraisal. For the line manager involved in appraising a headteacher 'a member of the Directorate' and the peer assessor 'the visiting headteacher' to work effectively together, their roles must be clarified. Appendix 13.6 shows how the roles are delineated.

Management of the scheme

It is envisaged that all teachers will be appraised approximately every two years. Copies of the Agreed Statement, which includes future targets and actions agreed at the appraisal interview will be held only by the appraisee, appraiser and headteacher. Copies of the self-evaluation and classroom observation notes may be attached to the Agreed Statement if the appraisee wishes. The Agreed Statements will be held for two complete appraisal cycles.

Appendix 13.1 Scottish nuclear staff performance appraisal and development scheme flowchart

1 APPRAISAL INTERVIEW
- Appraisal of performance in last 12 months
- Setting objectives for next 12 months
- Identification of training and development needs

2 FUTURE POTENTIAL REVIEW
- Review appraisal report
- Promotion potential assessment
- Long-term potential assessment

3 ACTING ON INFORMATION
- Developing appraisee in job
- Continuous informal monitoring
- Guidance and support
- Implementing specific action points

4 SIX MONTH REVIEW
- Interview to review original objectives
- Amendment/confirmation as appropriate
- Formal progress review

5 ACTING ON FURTHER INFORMATION
- Development
- Informal monitoring
- Guidance and support
- Action points

6 ISSUE OF NEXT APPRAISAL REPORT
- Documentation/instructions issued

CONTINUOUS APPRAISAL

Appendix 13.2   Scottish Nuclear staff performance
appraisal form

This form should be completed by the Appraiser during the Appraisal
Interview with the Appraisee. It should be signed and dated by both
parties and forwarded to the next Line Manager as soon as possible after
the interview has taken place, who, upon completion of all signatures at
Pt VII, should forward the form to the appropriate Personnel Manager. A
copy should be held by both the Appraiser and the Appraisee for reference
throughout the year.

PART I: CONFIRMATION OF PERSONAL DETAILS

Name: _____ Date of Appointment: _____

Location: _____ Date of Appointment
to present position: _____

Department: _____

Job title: _____

Job Grade: _____

Qualifications:
(Please underline any obtained in the last 12 months)

_____

_____

_____

_____

_____

CW27032,1

PART II: AGREED OBJECTIVES

FIXED OBJECTIVE AREAS

1. Efficiency Improvement:

_____

2. Quality Improvement:

_____

FLEXIBLE OBJECTIVE AREAS (In order of priority)

1.

_____

2.

_____

3.

_____

4.

_____

PART III: CORE SKILLS	*Appraiser's Comments*
1. Commitment	_____
2. Communication	_____
3. Professional Knowledge	_____
4. Decision Making	_____
5. Leadership	_____
6. Teamwork	_____
7. Management/Staff Development	_____
8. Innovation/Initiative	_____

PART IV: COMMENT ON ATTAINMENT   Performance
OF OBJECTIVES OVER LAST 12 MONTHS   Rating*

Low *1 2 3 4 5 6* High

_____   _____

_____   _____

_____   _____

_____   _____

_____   _____

_____

Comment over last 12 months

_____

_____   *1 2 = Does not meet requirement

_____   3 4 = Meets requirement

_____   5 6 = Exceeds requirement

_____

_____

_____

PART V: OVERALL PERFORMANCE ASSESSMENT

☐ A = Exceptional Performance

☐ B = Consistently High Level Performance

☐ C = Good Year's Work

☐ D = Some Shortcomings, Performance Otherwise Acceptable

☐ E = Performance Less Than Acceptable

PART VI: TRAINING REQUIRED TO MEET OBJECTIVES/IMPROVE
PERFORMANCE

PART VII: COMMENTS

(a) Appraiser:

(b) Appraisee:

SIGNED

APPRAISEE: _____ DATE: _____

APPRAISER: _____ DATE: _____

NEXT LINE MANAGER: _____ DATE: _____

Appendix 13.3   Headteacher appraisal – Process and timings (Fife Education Authority appraisal scheme)

Preliminary visit by director appraiser and visiting headteacher (up to 1 day)
(Familiarization with school. Uplifting of in-school
documentation – job description, curriculum documents, school
development plans, etc. Clarification and discussion of appraisal process.
Agreement of agenda for initial meeting. Agree total timetable.)

↓

General self-review by headteacher
(Consultation with a colleague. Input by teaching staff.)

↓

Meeting of director appraiser and visiting headteacher (up to $\frac{1}{2}$ day)
(Discussion of school documentation etc.
Agreement on possible areas of focus for initial meeting.)

↓

Initial meeting (up to 2 hours)
(Negotiation of areas of focus for appraisal and approaches/format
for specific self-review within those areas.
Negotiation of possible other sources of information.
Agreement of agenda for appraisal interview.)

↓

Written minute of initial meeting (up to 1 hour)
(Appraiser writes and sends to headteacher.)

↓

Specific self-review by headteacher

↓

Appraisal interview (up to 3 hours)
(Agreement on number/focus/phasing of targets and action plan.
Consideration of headteacher's professional
and personal development needs.)

↓

Draft statement to headteacher (up to 3 hours)
(Written by appraiser. Discussed with visiting headteacher
and sent to headteacher.)

↓

Agreed statement meeting (Time as required)
(Consideration of amendments. Signing. Commitment by appraiser
to positive support/resources for those areas in which he/she has
responsibility. Consideration of strategies. Setting of review date.)

↓

Debriefing meeting (up to 1 hour)
(Possible prior discussion with a colleague.
Consideration of the process.)

↓

Review (up to 2 hours)

Right-side timing brackets: 6 Weeks · 2 Days · 4–6 Weeks · 2 Weeks · 2–4 Weeks · 12 Months

Source: Fife Regional Council, Education Department (1991)

**Appendix 13.4   Class teacher appraisal – Process and timing
(Fife Education Authority appraisal scheme)**

Initial meeting (up to 1 hour)
(Clarification and discussion of appraisal
process and documentation.
Agreement of overall timetable.)

↓

Self-review (up to 2 hours)
(Using self-review form/prompt list.
Involving a colleague?)

AND

Classroom observation/s and feedback (up to 2 days)
(Planned observation/s. One general focus
plus one specific focus. Focus negotiated with appraisee.
Observation followed by immediate verbal feedback and
written summary. Possibility of peer observation.)

↓

Appraisal interview (up to 3 hours)
(Agenda largely based on self-review
form plus matters arising from
observations. Targets/action plan.)

↓

Draft statement to appraisee

↓

Agreed statement meeting (time as required)
(Consideration of amendments. Signing.
Commitment by appraiser to positive
support/resources for which he/she has
responsibility. Consideration of strategies.
Setting of review date.)

↓

Debriefing meeting (up to 1 hour)
(Consideration of the process.
Possible prior discussion with
a colleague.)

↓

Review (up to 2 hours)

4–6 Weeks

2 Weeks

2–4 Weeks

12 Months

Source: Fife Regional Council, Education Department (1991)

Appendix 13.5 Self-review form questions for Fife Education Authority appraisal scheme

The following questions are asked on the Fife Education Authority's appraisal scheme self-review form; space is given on the form for responses.

Please respond to following questions. They will form part of the agenda of the appraisal interview. Write in note form if you prefer. It would be helpful if you gave a copy to your appraiser before the appraisal interview but this is at your discretion. And you can ask for a copy to be attached to your appraisal documentation if you wish.

1. Which aspects of your work do you feel especially pleased with?

2. Which aspects of your job have not gone as well as you would have hoped?

3. Using the key task list as a prompt, are there any areas of your work you would like to take this opportunity to reflect on, write about and discuss?

4. Does your job description in fact describe what you do?

5. Are there any constraints or difficulties you are working under?

6. Do you feel you have strengths which are under-utilized within the school/Region?

7. What do you think should be the key aims in your work next year? Is there anything you would like to do which you do not have the opportunity to do now?

8. What hopes and aspirations do you have for your personal and professional future? What can be done in the next year and the longer term to develop your professional experience and add to your expertise?

Self-review prompt sheet – Key areas of management

The following headings may prove helpful when reflecting on aspects of your work.

Leadership

Establishing goals and priorities
Innovation and leadership
Communication, consultation, motivation
Setting standards

Monitoring and evaluation

Monitoring the learning environment
Evaluation of the learning and teaching process
Monitoring pupils' progress and support
Evaluation of staff development experiences
Monitoring class information procedures

Curriculum and assessment

Curriculum development and review
Assessment, reporting and recording procedures

Administration and management

Delegation/'fire fighting'
Time and stress management
Appointment, deployment and management of staff (teaching and non-teaching)
Finance control

Resource management/maintenance
General administration

Pupils' pastoral care

Effectiveness of procedures related to pupil welfare e.g. attendance, health, guidance, etc.
Discipline
Health and safety

Staff development and welfare

Staff development and appraisal procedures
Probationer support
Social and pastoral care of staff
Health and safety

Links with other agencies

Liaison with Directorate and Advisory Service
Liaison with other sectors
Parents and PTA
School Board
Health Service, Psychological Service, social work, etc.

Personal development

Contributions to regional and national developments
Continuous reflection/self-evaluation
Development of skills, knowledge and expertise

Self-review prompt sheet – Key areas of class teaching

The following headings may prove helpful when reflecting on aspects of your work.

Learning and teaching

Planning and preparation
Mastery and appropriate use of a variety of teaching styles
Organization of varied effective learning situations for the whole range of pupils
Setting and maintaining appropriate standards of work and presentation
Creating and maintaining an ordered and stimulating classroom environment
Classroom organization and management
Organization and deployment of appropriate resources
Assessing, recording and reporting pupil progress

Curriculum

Primary/special

Language
Mathematics/Practical activities
Environmental studies
Expressive arts
Social and religious education

Secondary

Range of subjects
Stages
Abilities
National certification
Personal and social development

Pastoral

Overview of pupil welfare and progress
Contribution to social development

Whole school

Contribution to school/curriculum development
Contribution to the wider life of the school

Liaison/communication

- with management
- with colleagues
- with parents
- with support services
- with outside agencies
- with community

Personal development

Evaluation of own teaching
Continuous development of own skills, knowledge and expertise

Source: Fife Regional Council, Education Department (1991)

Appendix 13.6   The roles of director and visiting headteacher in the headteacher appraisal process (Fife Education Authority appraisal scheme)

The importance of understanding the roles of the director appraiser and visiting headteacher in the appraisal process cannot be over-emphasized. The key elements of these two roles are summarized below.

Director appraiser	Visiting headteacher
Initiates contact with appraisee in writing and provides draft timetable of process.	Accompanies Director Appraiser on the school visit.
Chairs all the meetings relating to the process including the appraisal interview.	Assists in assembling and considering documentation and preparing agenda.
Agrees outcomes with headteacher and actions appropriate support.	Is present at all meetings except the Agreed Statement meeting and the review.
Writes the Agreed Statement and summary of meetings.	Provides professional advice and support as appropriate at all meetings attended.
	In the interests of confidentiality the visiting headteacher can be asked to withdraw when issues relating to personal matters are discussed at the appraisal interview.
	Will not be present at Agreed Statement meeting.

Source: Fife Regional Council, Education Department (1991)

Index